EASTER EGGS

EASTER EGGS

A Collector's Guide

by
Victor Houart

SOUVENIR PRESS

First published 1978 by Souvenir Press Ltd,
43 Great Russell Street, London WC1B 3PA
and simultaneously in Canada

ISBN 0 285 62322 2

Filmset and printed in Great Britain by
BAS Printers Limited, Over Wallop, Hampshire.

Book designed by Pamela Mara

TABLE OF CONTENTS

ACKNOWLEDGEMENTS

This book could not have been written without the kind help and assistance of many people, scattered all over the European continent, who not only provided me with valuable information on such little documented subjects as Easter eggs and Easter customs, but also supplied me with a rich harvest of photographs. Researches into the history of the Easter egg understandably covered a vast area and I was forced to get in touch with people who were as unknown to me as I was to them. Yet the fact that we were strangers in no way prevented them from helping me. Indeed, taking into account the distances and the language difficulties involved, I was constantly astonished by the degree of goodwill and understanding I encountered, and the amount of trouble scholars were prepared to take to answer my questions.

I had thus the pleasure of discovering that kind people who love their jobs or simply love their neighbours, even when they are miles apart, still exist in this modern world, as was proved to me by the following persons, all of whom I want to thank most warmly:
Dr Winifred Baer, Staatlichen Schlosser im Garten, Charlottenburg Castle, Berlin; John C. Baker, of the Sunderland Museum; Christian Baulez, Curator at the Versailles Museum; Prof Dr Hadjinikolov, Director of Ethnographic Museum, Sofia, Bulgaria; Janos Hidasi of Hungexport, Budapest; Kati Idranij, from Budapest; Prof Dr Erich Kollmann, of Cologne; Catherine Lagrue, of the Angers Museum; A. R. Mountford, Director of Museums, Stoke-On-Trent; Mrs Nowakowska and Mr Jan Sek, of the Polish Interpress Agency; Dr Jaroslav Orel, of Brno, Czechoslovakia; Mrs Kenneth Snowman, of Wartski's, London; Miss Straesser, Curator of the Herbig-Haarhaus Lackmuseum, in Cologne; Mr G. Tikholaz, vice-president of the Ukrainian Friendship Society, Kiev, USSR; Mrs Robert Villers, of the Lambinet Museum in Versailles; Dr Leonie von Wilckens, Curator of the Germanisches National Museum, Nuremberg; Mr & Mrs Wery, of Liège, Dr Günter Schade, director of Staatliche Museen, Berlin, DDR.

PREFACE

I am a great traveller although I hardly leave my house. But then I have only to shut my eyes to start journeying down time to a tiny hidden universe which, for many years past, has taken the form of an island floating gently in space. It is the faraway kingdom of my childhood: nothing grander than a small village which will remain unchanged forever. These visions are guarded by ten tall poplars, and kind people, gentle animals, cheeky birds, colourful flowers, strange insects, are busy between fairy-tale farmhouses, dusty sunken roads which lead to unknown destinations, and peaceful hills of black, fertile earth. It was indeed a village full of marvels.

Although we had never been to school we could decipher weather signs in the sky. We knew the names of all the trees, the songs of all the birds and, above all, we had all been acquainted early with the facts of life and the dramatic story of the life and death of all species. We were all familiar, without any calendar to help us, with the rules of the passing of time under the inexorable sun. We could tell that Easter was coming because we had seen but one flower in a field or some buds on the willow-trees by the river. That was the time when the women of the village started cleaning houses from top to bottom, scrubbing, polishing, moving furniture, painting window-frames, as if they were rigging a tall invisible ship.

At night, we were told the sad story of some poor, long-haired Jew called Jesus, who had been arrested in a town called Jerusalem. We were never spared the gruesome details of the iniquitous judgment, the terrible flogging and the cruel crucifixion. For three long days the church bells fell silent and we could feel the tension growing. The bells had gone to Rome, a big town lost somewhere on the planet, far beyond our poplars.

The shock always came on Sunday when the bells, back from their pilgrimage, started ringing again and eggs fell from the sky among the tulips and the daffodils. We were, I remember, in a real sense little barbarians, for an egg in that kingdom of ours, dyed or not, decorated or not, was always associated in our minds with the mystery of creation. Inside was the seed of life. And we all knew it.

That peaceful and innocent world is now gone forever, sunken with all its treasures deep in my memory. The beautiful spring festival of long ago has turned out to be nothing more than a long week-end, an opportunity to desert for three days our monstrous concrete world from which nature has been banned, and to race along busy roads searching in vain for a promised land which perhaps does not exist.

But despite the secularisation of the ancient Easter traditions, and our carelessness of the God of the Christians, the sun god of our ancestors or any other gods, people in Europe, urged by some deep-rooted barbarian instinct, still give Easter eggs to their children. Today, the gift of an egg does not carry the deep symbolic meaning it once had, and few people realise that they are taking part in a ritual that goes back thousands of years. Yet the giving of the Easter egg remains a beautiful antique gesture, to be renewed every year when the sun rises again on a new spring.

THE EGG IN THE ANTIQUE WORLD

~~~~~~

Among all the pagan symbols, the origins of which are lost in the mists of time but which have somehow been transmitted to us by our barbarian ancestors, that of the egg has remained apparently indestructible. It has been beyond the power of the church, and of political, philosophical or social movements to suppress, so that today the custom of giving eggs at Easter, or, as I prefer to call it, the spring equinox, is as popular as ever. In a sense, the tradition might be said to be regaining its old symbolic value, in that it has been able to disentangle itself, perhaps mainly in communist countries, from the overlay of centuries of Christianity.

The Christian church has always had a knack of assimilating pagan symbols and pagan feasts and transforming them so that the original meaning is often lost. In the case of the egg, the church inherited a tradition that goes back to our remotest ancestors. It was for instance a powerful symbol for all the nations of the Middle East, in the very corner of the world where some of the first civilisations sprang into being.

The secret development of a germ inside a fragile eggshell impressed and frightened the early men. The egg was the symbol of creation, of life itself. The invisible action inside the closed shell, which, unattended by any external influence, after a mysteriously fixed period leads to birth, inspired the first men with a deep religious respect. Men and women alike stood in awe before that perfect microcosm in which the mystery of the creation of life was repeated again and again.

The sacred egg was introduced early in the cosmogony of the ancient Egyptians, who gave the principles of genesis a central place in their religious cycles. Among the friendly powers of the earth, the Egyptians worshipped the creative force which stocked the universe with living marvels. And as a symbol of that divine force, they chose the egg. They placed it, because it contained the divine principle of a spontaneous generation, at the beginning of their genesis cycle. The egg was the universal germ, the original cell which exploded under the influence of an unidentified force, giving birth to the universe. It was, as we put it today, the 'big bang'.

And the priests of Egypt, like those of the Phoenicians and the Carthaginians after them, refused to eat eggs, so that they would not offend the creative powers by destroying a germ of life. The same attitude was adopted later by the followers of Orpheus and Pythagoras, and it has often been recorded that, as late as the eighteenth century, the Moors and Berbers still refused to eat eggs.

The Egyptian civilisation was not the only one to choose the egg as a symbol: practically all ancient civilisations adopted it. India also taught the myth of the universal egg, and it is probable that many of the Brahmin beliefs proceed from some recollections of the ancient Egyptian dogmas. The Indian genesis story explains that at the beginning the primitive germ was in a state of suspension and that its mass was initially shapeless. It later condensed into an egg shining like gold and full of light. Brahma, father of all spirits, was born in that shell and here he lived for a long period of time, the creative force imprisoned. Finally the shell broke by itself, the upper part forming the sky, the lower part the Earth, with the air in between. Just as it happened in Egypt, the egg became in India the symbol of the universal germ.

The Chaldeans and the Persians, in fact all the people of Aryan origin, chose the bull as the symbol of the cosmic force. The creation myths of those civilisations taught that matter first took the shape of an egg and that the bull Abudad broke the shell with one of its horns, giving birth to living creatures. In the sacred books of Zoroastra, the egg appears as a universe where two principles, Ormuzd the good and Rhiman the evil, are in continual conflict with each other.

The miracle of creation — an ostrich egg being hatched in the hot desert sun. In the Middle Ages, the ostrich egg was seen by the theologians as a symbol of Christ's resurrection by God the Father.

Ormuzd, the victor, finally created an immense egg which gave birth to the twenty-four auxiliary gods.

The Phoenicians and the Assyrians, it seems, gave to the egg a less profound significance, it being only the symbol of the terrestrial globe. This may be why the Phoenicians and the Carthaginians, two great maritime nations, painted ostrich eggs with geometrical motifs, lotus flowers or palms. But nobody knows what these eggs, many of which have been excavated, were used for.

Even the faraway Chinese taught the myth of the universal egg. Puonsu, the Adam of the Chinese, was born from an egg which preceded the creation of the universe. The shell of that original egg formed the sky, the white became the air and the yellow yolk gave birth to plants and animals.

Nearer to us, Greece adopted many myths and beliefs from the ancient Egyptians and among them the dogma of the original egg, principle of the universe. This is the guiding principle of the philosopher Thales. Original chaos, a shapeless assembly of cosmic matter, condensed into the shape of an egg. Orpheus calls the first man 'son of the egg'.

Unfortunately, the sacred egg of the beginning of the Greek civilisation degenerated in due course into a simple offering to the gods in the course of religious ceremonies. It is recorded that in Sparta, for instance, an egg was hung in a temple near the tomb of Castor, reminding wayfarers of the miraculous birth and origin of Castor, Pollux, Clytemnestra and Helen of Troy, sons and daughters of Zeus and Leda. Having once and for all discarded the primitive symbol of the egg, the Greeks used eggs as sacrifices to the deities and placed them on the altars of their temples.

There was but one more step to take. And it was the Persians who, remembering the ancient traditions of the *ovum zoroastrum*, innovated the practice of exchanging eggs, usually painted in red, at the time of the spring equinox, when huge feasts were organised. Those Persians eggs are therefore the most ancient examples of our Easter eggs. And the custom has never disappeared in Iran. Today, village people still exchange eggs painted red or mauve at the time of the spring equinox, which also marks the beginning of the Iranian new year.

THE ROMANS AND THE RISE
OF CHRISTIANITY

It was a Roman writer, Horace, who invented the expression *ab ovo*, 'starting with the egg', referring to the egg of Leda from which sprang Helen of Troy. But the Romans, though successors of the Greeks, had no feeling for the deepest antique significance of the egg. For them, it was a straightforward symbol of nature's fecundity. Eggs were broken in Rome to ward off evil spells and to induce immunity to various calamities. The young men of Rome sometimes used eggs in the course of initiation games. But at the end they always broke them, to repel evil spirits. The most important Roman festivity, the feast of Ceres, which was held in April (more or less at the time of our Easter or the spring equinox), did make use of eggs, showing therefore that the ancient traditions had not been completely lost; and like other peoples had done before them, the Romans also placed eggs in tombs beside their dead, and very often gave funeral caskets an oval shape.

This association with death, the original meaning of which seems to be completely lost, was observed by the Carthaginians, and probably, by still more ancient peoples since traces of it have been found in many parts of Europe. The earliest decorated egg known is probably an ostrich egg, now in the Granada Museum, which was discovered during the excavation of a bronze age burial ground. Eggs have been discovered in several Slavic tombs in Moravia, which date from a later period, probably the eleventh century. In Germany, the most ancient decorated egg was discovered in the Romano-Germanic sarcophagus of a little girl, in Worms. It is a goose egg, fully decorated, which goes back approximately to the fourth century. In Hungary, such eggs, painted and decorated, have been discovered in various tombs of the Avars, those tribes from Asia who ravaged parts of Europe for three hundred years before they were halted at the end of the eighth century.

The mysterious link between eggs and the dead has survived into quite recent times, for not so long ago, the Russians used to visit cemeteries on Easter Sunday to hang eggs from the branches of the crosses, exactly as if they had wanted to share the joys of spring with their dead.

Archaeological excavations carried out in Poland have unearthed still another custom involving eggs, which has a definite Slavic origin. In Obole and in Danzig, decorated eggs of earthenware and stone have been found under ancient dwellings. In both cases, they were embellished with geometrical motifs and were also engraved. Historians believe that these were offerings to the domestic spirits, the egg being again seen as the symbol of concealed life developing inside the shell.

And the conquered Celts of Western Europe, whose religion is not even today well understood because their culture was so brutally eradicated, first by the Romans and later by the Christians, also had a certain mystical belief in the egg. Ancient Gallic traditions mention a sacred egg, 'the egg of the Druids', the famous *anguinum* which frightened the Roman soldiers and which is connected with the snake, as it was in Egypt.

The old Druids, the witch doctors of the Celtic tribes, are credited with originating the snake-egg legend. They declared that the snake-egg proceeded from the saliva of the snake during copulation, and that the owner of such an egg would be protected against thunder, against the 'fire of the sky', and against mortal wounds. The two gods Teutales and Esus would give him protection in combat and make him victorious. As the main enemies of the Celts were in fact the Romans, one can understand the apprehension of the latter.

Rome started to decline at the same time as Christianity was gaining a firm hold in Western Europe. All the ancient pagan symbols and customs were forbidden. At the beginning, even the celebration of the winter solstice and the spring equinox, two deeply embedded pagan feasts, were banned, until the church, realising its mistake, transformed the occasions into Christmas and Easter. The new church, with a fine insight into psychology, chose not to forbid the old religious practices, but rather to take them over and give them an altogether different meaning.

When Pope Gregory the Great sent missionaries to Britain, he instructed them 'not to destroy the idols, but to spray them with holy water'. Missionaries were advised to build their churches in the pagan temples: examples of such substitutions exist throughout Europe. It was a very effective strategy. The angels and the saints duly replaced the gods and the heroes. Saint Michael took over from Mercury.

So the egg, ancient symbol of creation, though first tolerated by the Christian church, had then to be 'Christianised'. Easter, the old feast of the spring equinox, became the feast of the resurrection of Christ, a feast which falls on the first Sunday after the full moon which follows the spring equinox. And it was Saint Augustine who decided that the egg should represent the resurrection of Christ, a feature of Christian belief that has been encouraged ever since. The pagan symbol and the spring feast have been smoothly taken over as if their original meaning had never existed. And throughout the centuries, people have eaten eggs at Easter, but blessed ones now, and offered eggs to their children and friends, with an almost total unawareness of the gesture's once cosmic significance.

The word 'Easter'

According to an English historian of the eighth century, the Venerable Bede, the word Easter derives from the Norse *Ostara* or *Eostre*, meaning 'festival of spring'. The word for Easter in all Germanic languages, except Dutch, has the same etymology. All the Latin languages on the other hand use a word which derives from the Hebrew, such as *Pâques* in French or *Pascuas* in Spanish. In the Hebrew language, the word *Pashuah* means 'crossing'. And it is a fact that the Jews celebrate, at the spring equinox, not the resurrection of Christ, but the crossing of the Red Sea and the exodus from Egypt by the tribes of Israel.

EASTER EGGS OF THE MIDDLE AGES

~~~~~~

Nobody knows exactly what happened in Europe between the great barbarian invasions, which led to the fall of the Roman Empire, and the beginning of the Middle Ages, a period which covers more or less six centuries. Historians call that period 'the Dark Ages'. Europe appeared to fall into a kind of deep sleep; documents from that period of time are very scarce indeed. What really happened to the Easter customs in the Dark Ages no one knows for sure. But it is well established that as early as the eleventh century, children would go from house to house collecting eggs at Easter.

In those days, the long forty-day fast of Lent, during which time the eating of eggs was forbidden by the church, ended in a festival. Starting on Good Friday the students and the choir boys traditionally congregated in all the public squares, where a procession was formed. Then, preceded by trumpets, drums and banners, they made their way to the main church before which they sang hymns. Afterwards they dispersed through all the streets of the town in order to collect eggs from house to house. Standing in front of each house, the children and the students would sing traditional or satirical songs, and the eggs collected were used to cook huge omelettes to be eaten with family or friends. This custom remained alive in many regions until the Second World War, and the French still remember a few of the songs which originated in the Middle Ages:

> 'Wake up, you men,
> Men who are asleep.
> Have you got some
> Or haven't you any?'

The children of the province of Bresse used to sing:

'O girls and women who are making custards,
Do not put all your eggs in them.
Give me two, you'll go to heaven,
Give me three, you'll go there right away!'

In the valley of the Loire river, mainly in the region of Château-Chinon, children with egg-baskets under their arms sang:

'Give an egg to those little children.
For you they'll say *De profundis*,
Which will take you straight to Paradise.'

In other regions the song went:

'Take the key of your cupboard,
Give us eggs, please,
Give us whatever you like.
Alleluia!'

But of course, some doors did not open, so the children who did not receive the expected eggs had another song ready to fit the occasion:

'I'll go as I came
Has your hen not laid any egg?
Or is it you who are a miser,
Alleluia!'

In certain regions of Europe, for the customs varied from place to place, peasants on Easter Saturday used to take baskets full of eggs to church to get them blessed by the priest, who kept some, either for himself or to distribute among the congregation after the Easter Mass.

This practice of giving away huge quantities of eggs just before Easter, which is mentioned in numerous documents from the Middle Ages onwards, had a basically economic character. When Lent was strictly kept, and for forty days the eating of eggs (among other produce) was forbidden, but no interdiction prevented the hens from continuing to lay, huge quantities of eggs were accumulated in all the farms of Christendom. By Easter, farmers were rather glad to get rid of their stocks as quickly as possible.

In England, where the egg ritual was less strictly observed than on

16

the Continent, it was the custom instead to offer on Good Friday 'hot cross buns', small spicy loaves of bread bearing the trace of a cross. This custom too goes back to the Middle Ages, and is reputed to have started at St Alban's Abbey, where the first pilgrims would be welcomed by the monks with 'cross buns'.

The custom of egg-collecting at the approach of Easter, which is at least a thousand years old, continued through war, plague or other calamities and is still revived now and then in villages across Christian Europe. The eggs which were collected, blessed and eaten at Easter during the Middle Ages were all natural, and had been laid by hens, though other types, such as duck eggs, were also used. They were simply dyed, and sometimes decorated with primitive designs by enterprising village artists. Nobody it seems ever thought at that time to produce artificial Easter eggs – a pity for collectors perhaps.

However, there was one innovation during that period of our history: the first ostrich eggs started to appear in Western Europe during the thirteenth century, and they were soon to take part in the Easter celebrations.

OSTRICH EGGS

W̲e know today that ostrich eggs, to which were attributed certain magical powers by medieval Europeans, first appeared in Western Europe some time during the thirteenth century. They were probably brought back by the first navigators who visited North Africa, although the Crusaders may also have been responsible. It is from a study of the ancient inventories of collections assembled during the Middle Ages that we learn that ostrich eggs were regarded as a rare and always an expensive curiosity. In his *Glossaire Archéologique du Moyen-Âge et de la Renaissance*, the French historian, Victor Gay, mentions a series of ostrich eggs, mostly kept in the treasuries of cathedrals and churches, the most ancient of which is described in the *Thes. Sedis Apostolica No 321*, as mounted on silver and dating from 1295. The text is as follows: '*Unam enpam de ovo strucii cum circulo et sbarris et pede rotundo de argento, in quo sunt quatuor bestie aliquantulum relevate. Interius antem est guarnita de argento*'. (An egg shell encircled by a band and bars, and a circular base on which are engraved four beasts in low relief. The front interior is ornamented with silver.)

Other ancient documents confirm the presence of ostrich eggs in Europe at a very early date. One entry in the inventory of Raoul de Clermont, a French nobleman, dated 1302, says: '*une cope d'oeuf d'oustruce, guernie d'or bien doré, pesant $3\frac{1}{2}M$*' (One ostrich egg cup, decorated with gold, weighing $3\frac{1}{2}$ marcs).[1] Another inventory dating from 1397, mentioned by Dehaisnes in his book *Documents concernant l'histoire du Moyen-Âge*, contains an entry which says: '*item um oef d'osterisse bordet d'argent, vaut V francs*' (item an ostrich egg with silver border, value 5 francs).

---

[1] Marc: ancient French measure equivalent to eight ounces, or 244,75 grammes.

18

An ostrich egg from the Middle Ages, probably 14th century, now in the Angers Museum, in France.

In the inventory of the possessions of Charles V, king of France (1338–1380), made immediately after his death, there is a mention of 'various ostrich egg cups'. His son King Charles VI's inventory, taken in 1399, refers on page 366 to still another cup the basin of which is an ostrich egg. But most of the ostrich eggs are mentioned in the inventories of the treasures of numerous cathedrals and churches, where they were used in the Easter ritual. We know for instance that the church of Cambrai, in Northern France, was in possession of 'four ostrich eggs decorated with silver in various ways', and that the cathedral of Angers had, in 1467, 'two big ostrich eggs to be used at Easter'. The same entry appears in the inventories taken in 1539, 1595 and as late as 1606. In the 1596 inventory one reads *'item, deux oeufs d'autruche qui servent à donner les oeufs de Pâques'* (Item, two ostrich eggs which are used to give the Easter eggs), a confusing text as one cannot imagine how the ostrich eggs were used to provide other eggs. But the presence of eggs in Angers cathedral is confirmed in an inventory taken during the eighteenth century, in which it is stated that there are two ostrich eggs in the great reliquary, suspended on silver chains. On Easter Sunday these eggs were apparently displayed on the altar of Saint Réné.

During the fifteenth century, the presence of ostrich eggs was reported in numerous churches in all regions and most of those eggs remained in these holy buildings until well into the eighteenth century. The 1511 inventory of Avignon cathedral is very explicit, for it says: *'tria ova altratura munita cathenis et ligaminibus argenteis et cum armis sanctissimi papae Julii cum un minoribus esset archiepiscopa et legati avinionensis'*. (Three ostrich eggs provided with chains and attachments in silver, ornamented with the coat of arms of the Holy Lord, Pope Jules, who at the time was archbishop and legate in Avignon). And one can read the following in the inventory of Noyon cathedral, dated 1523: *'ova dua magna alba, quorum unum est ligatur laminis seu bendis argenteis et cupio orificum est obditum argento, in quo sunt multa fragmenta de Innocentibus'*. (Two big white eggs, one of which is held by small bars and a band in silver, the opening of which is covered by a silver cupola, containing relics of the Innocents).

In fact there is no end to the list of ostrich eggs recorded in churches in France, in the Low Countries, in Germany and elsewhere, during the Middle Ages. They were hung from church ceilings, in the manner of the ancient Greeks who hung eggs from the ceilings of their temples. Perhaps this represented some sort of pagan memory in the minds of the priests, who also used the eggs as containers for the relics of saints.

Both those practices are confirmed by many ancient texts, one of which, written in 1372, states that 'one hangs up ostrich eggs in churches for their excellence, their size and because they are very scarce in the country'. And in 1556, Cardanus, the Italian philosopher, could write in his book *Inventions*, that 'those eggs are as big as a child's head, round, and when they are old they look like ivory. It is the custom to hang them up in temples, for, due to their hardness, they last a very long time and when their humour is evaporated they get as hard as bones'.

The inventory of St-Omer cathedral, written in 1557, records that the cathedral had 'two ostrich eggs containing various bones

Persian ostrich egg, engraved with Arabic lettering and motifs. Middle of the 19th century. *Courtesy Victoria and Albert Museum, London*

and relics'. And the inventory of the Church St Nicaise in Rheims, dated 1640, states that the church possesses 'an ostrich egg containing the relics of St Benôit, St Thierry, St Aman and the saints Crispin and Crespinian'.

If the ancient civilisations saw in the egg the symbol of life and creation, the theologians of the Middle Ages saw in the ostrich egg the symbol of Christ being resurrected by God the Father. The choice of the ostrich, a bird hardly known to the Europeans of the time, held a special meaning, for the ostrich is the only bird that leaves its eggs in the sand to be hatched by the heat of the sun. The Catholic Church thus adopted ostrich eggs as symbols of a miracle, and displayed them in churches and cathedrals on Good Friday and on Easter Sunday.

The ostrich egg was associated very early with the Easter ritual. Reverend Vincelot, a learned French priest, wrote the following in his etymological essays on the ornithology of Maine: 'On Easter Sunday, in Angers cathedral, two clergymen called *corbeillers*, or basket-bearers, had to go into the church vestry, immediately after matins, put the amice on their heads, a square flat cap on the amice, and dress themselves with an alb, embroidered gloves, a belt and a dalmatic before going, without any stole, to the tomb. There each picked up a small basin containing an ostrich egg covered with white material and proceeded with them to the bishop's throne. The oldest of them had to present his ostrich egg to the bishop and say in a low voice *"Surrexit Dominus, Alleluia!"* (The lord has risen, Alleluia!) And the bishop then answered: *"Deo Gratias, Alleluia!"*

'What the oldest basket-bearer had done on the right side of the bishop was done on the left side by the other. And both of them had then to go round all the church, to convey an identical message to all the clergymen present and receive the same answer. Then the ostrich eggs were taken back to the vestry.'

Reverend Vincelot added that he had seen, in the Monplacet church in the Loire valley, a suspended ostrich egg. It is still there, the only ostrich egg which has remained in its place since the Middle Ages.

In many places ostrich eggs were used as accessories in the liturgical dramas played in the open ground in front of churches at Easter. These included the Drama of the Three Maries or the Drama of the Resurrection of Christ. There is a reference to this practice in the *Grande Bible Des Noëls Angevins* (Great Bible of the Christmas Carols of Anjou), written by Urbain Renard, a French historian, in 1780. The following carol found in the book is very explicit:

> 'It is a perfect joy
> At Easter to hear
> Bells, organs, music,
> To see the Maries,
> Look in the sepulchre
> For Christ who is not there.
> Then, carrying ostrich eggs,
> To sing alleluia!'

However, from the sixteenth century, when the religious fervour of the Middle Ages had gradually declined, the ostrich eggs ceased to be the exclusive or near-exclusive property of the churches. In time they became expensive and rare curiosities which, richly mounted, found their way into the many *cabinets d'amateurs* of the Renaissance. These were mounted, everywhere in Europe but mainly in Germany and in France, in gold, silver, coral, or even in silver gilt. Today, ostrich eggs dating from before the end of the eighteenth century are very scarce, and when one of them surfaces at an auction, it sells for a considerable price. In any case most of them, being very fragile, are damaged in some way or other. A very rare example of a sixteenth-century ostrich egg is preserved in Corpus Christi College, Cambridge University, to which it was left in the will of Richard Fletcher, Bishop of Bristol, later of London, in 1594. The bishop's will is dated 25 October 1593 and the egg is a year older. It is described in the will as 'one estridges egg'. It has three plain straps and is supported on a stem formed from a twisted tree trunk resting on a reef-shaped pedestal. It is $11\frac{5}{8}$ inches in diameter and the base is $4\frac{3}{4}$ inches. What makes it unusual is the fact that the upper part, forming the cover, comes from the egg of a North African ostrich, while the lower part comes from the egg of a South African one.

It must be mentioned here that while ostrich eggs were extremely popular in Germany in the late sixteenth and seventeenth centuries, they were exceedingly rare in Britain. Yet there are records of the existence of another ostensibly British egg, which once belonged to

Rare English silver mounted ostrich egg belonging to Corpus Christi College, University of Cambridge. It was left to the university by Richard Fletcher, bishop of Bristol, later of Worcester and London, in his will dated 25th October 1593. The mounted egg is a year older. *Photograph by Edward Leigh, Cambridge*

the Randolph Hearst collection, but whose present whereabouts are unknown. The cup is lavishly mounted on silver gilt, with ornaments typical of the period; and the egg is supported by three caryatid figures. The finial is a figure of Minerva holding a banner which is inscribed on one side in the pleasant lettering of the time: 'The 4th October 1557, Mr John Stopes came to be our parson.' It is engraved also with a figure of Mary Magdalene.

This ostrich egg cup was in fact offered by his parishioners to John Stopes, as explained by the text engraved on the lip of the cup, which runs as follows: 'This cup was given to Mr John Stopes, our parsonns sonne by the parishioners of the parish of St Mary Magdalen in or neere Old Fishstreet London for his paines taking with us by his often preaching with us, hoping that he will so friendly accept it as most franckly and willing meane it. The first day of January 1623'. John Stopes was educated at Pembroke College, Cambridge and took orders at Oxford in 1609. He became curate of St Mary Magdalen, in Old Fish Street, London, a church that was destroyed by the Great Fire of London in 1666. It should be noted that the ostrich egg cup was offered to John Stopes on the first day of January 1623: the new Gregorian calendar had not yet been adopted in England, so the first day of January still corresponded more or less to the spring equinox.

Many famous ostrich egg cups are found in museums, such as the rather extraordinary example in the Kunsthistorische Museum of Vienna. It is not, one has to admit, an Easter egg proper. It is a piece of table sculpture, decorated with large pieces of coral, standing out like leafless trees, an example of that eccentric taste in embellishment which has seldom been practised outside Germany. The cup was wrought by Augsburg craftsmen at the end of the sixteenth century, at about the time enamel was introduced. The egg itself is mounted on the back of an enamelled ostrich which is led by a young negro slave, also enamelled.

In the eighteenth century, craftsmen developed still another technique, that of engraving the ostrich eggs with various scenes, a very delicate task which requires enormous skill. A typical example of this technique is to be found on an egg in the collection of the Staatliche Kunstsamnlungen Museum of Kassel, in Germany. It is an unmounted ostrich egg engraved in 1726 for the *landgrave* Karl of

Hesse. Meticulously worked, an unknown artist has engraved it with the figures of Vulcan and Venus underneath the Hesse coat of arms, with two flower garlands and two cupids holding the monogram 'L.C.'.

But all those magnificent ostrich egg cups, the most ancient of which date from the Middle Ages, and all the beautiful examples which were mounted by the goldsmiths of the sixteenth and seventeenth centuries, are extremely hard to come by today and most of them reach fabulous prices in auction rooms. One can only hope to discover later examples, such as those which were mounted on silver, mostly in Germany, at the end of the eighteenth century.

Of course, it should be remembered that ostrich egg cups were also produced during the nineteenth century, and these later examples should not be regarded as unworthy of a good collection. The Parisian firm of Barbedienne, for instance, produced some beautiful examples between 1870 and 1880. The Barbedienne ostrich eggs were given a coat of lacquer in the Japanese manner, as Japanese art, which finally gave birth to the *fin de siècle* style, was in the process of being 'discovered' in Europe at the time. One may also find, with a bit of luck, Easter ostrich eggs decorated with icons in faraway monasteries in Ethiopia.

Ostrich egg cups, much rarer than the coconut cups of the same period, were still natural, even if they were sometimes lavishly mounted. Until the middle of the eighteenth century hardly any artificial Easter egg, nor any surprise egg containing sweets or jewels, nor even a single egg in gold or other precious metal had been produced. (However, it is reported that Easter eggs in ceramic were produced in the Ukraine, between the tenth and thirteenth centuries.) That was mainly a nineteenth-century fashion, and even when artificial eggs were the vogue among the nobility, it never stopped peasants in France, Macedonia, Serbia, Poland, Bohemia or Russia and elsewhere from continuing to dye, decorate and offer to their relatives and friends just plain natural eggs, on Easter Sunday.

EIGHTEENTH-CENTURY EASTER EGGS AND THE FRENCH COURT

~~~~~~

At the end of the seventeenth century artificial Easter eggs did not exist – outside the Ukraine at least, although one over-zealous writer did report having seen them in Spain. Only natural eggs were used at Easter, usually coloured with vegetable dyes. The idea of decorating eggs to make them more attractive evolved towards the end of the seventeenth century, and it is certain that the French were involved in this development. It is thanks to the writings of Louis de Rouvroy, Duke of St Simon, author of the famous *Memoires* in which he told of the thousand and one incidents of Louis XIV's court and penned portraits of the great personalities of his time, that we know what happened at Versailles at Easter time. The Sun King appears to have liked the traditional folklore of Easter, and every year of his reign, enormous baskets containing pyramids of eggs were laid out in the king's chamber. These dyed or coloured eggs were eagerly blessed by the court chaplain and then distributed by the king to his near relatives, as well as to his guards and servants. It seems that it was Louis XIV who first had the idea of having eggs painted with various scenes, and the story is told that he offered a holy relic placed inside an egg to Madame de Lavallière, his charming favourite of the time, who entered a Carmelite convent in 1674.

The royal custom established under Louis XIV was retained at the French court, and was also followed in a large number of French stately homes until the end of the eighteenth century. It died out only under Louis XVI, to the great displeasure of the farmers in the Versailles neighbourhood, who for generations had sold eggs at Easter time to the courtiers, who in turn had offered them to the king and the royal princes.

Under Louis XV, at the height of a period of great refinement, the eggs destined for the king and members of the royal family were actually painted, as reported in some French documents, by such

German ostrich egg mounted on silver. Second half of 18th century.

famous artists as Boucher, Watteau and Lancret, but these works of art have long since disappeared, if they ever existed. Also, it is not commonly known that Versailles had a small zoo, that the ostrich eggs farmed there were used for other things than making omelettes, and that there was even an official painter more or less attached to the zoo who painted, sometimes with difficulty, the ostrich eggs

27

destined to be given to the king at Easter. The name of the painter, Jean-Etienne Lebel, would surely never have been passed down to posterity had he not carried out this humble work.

Poor Lebel had several worries of his own. At that time in France no one could be accepted as a master painter without belonging to the painters' guild. For example, only the members of the Royal Academy, to which Lebel did not belong, had the right to organise exhibitions of their works. It was only with the greatest difficulty that the Academy of St Luc, to which Lebel became an adviser, managed to organise seven exhibitions during the course of the eighteenth century. In a letter dated 3 April 1760, a certain Mr Delaroche intervened on Lebel's behalf with the Marquis de Marigny, Abel François Poisson, brother of the Marquise de Pompadour, who had obtained leave to succeed Le Normand de Tournehem as head of the *Direction Générale des Bâtiments*, equivalent to a ministry of arts today. In this letter, which has never before been published, Delaroche explains: 'I have the honour to beg you with the greatest entreaty to be pleased to accord your kindness to Master Lebel, painter. He is the man who has for the past ten years been painting the ostrich eggs at the small zoo. He would desire a privilege for working independently and for not being troubled in his work. This young fellow is well-behaved and has talent. The king has found his eggs very prettily painted. As a painter he has taken the respectful liberty of writing four verses on an Easter egg in the form of a petition in which he explains his request for a privilege. The king has read it and appeared to approve'.

In the Grand Trianon of Versailles two ostrich eggs remain, one of which was unfortunately partly broken about 1835. Both of them are mounted on tripods and presented in the form of perfume urns, with three ornate ramsheads' handles in ebony and box-wood. A third Easter ostrich egg from the royal collection is also kept in Versailles, and has managed to escape the ravages of time. It is mounted on ivory and wood of the pomegranate tree, and it is said that Madame Adelaide, Louis XVIII's aunt, personally turned the ivory. This beautiful egg is decorated with a scene representing a gathering in a park and is a demonstration of Lebel's talent.

There probably exists in a private collection another Easter egg painted by the same artist, and which belonged at one time to Louis XV. At the dedication of the St Luc Academy in Paris on 22 August 1774, there is mention of the presence of an ostrich egg decorated with a carnival scene painted by Lebel. On 1 December 1932 at the sale of the Blumenthal collection, an ostrich egg was in fact sold which was said to have belonged to Louis XV, and which was decorated with a carnival scene. It is reasonable to think that this was indeed the Easter egg from the St Luc Academy.

The French court also introduced 'surprise eggs', artificial eggs containing presents, a practice which has remained popular until the present day. The Lambinet Museum of Versailles, which has inherited certain objects from the royal collections saved from the revolutionaries, owns among other things two surprise eggs, probably the most amusing and interesting of all the eggs which passed through the French court. They were gifts to Madame Victoire, aunt of Louis XVI, at Easter 1783. These two eggs, which are not ostrich eggs as reported by some historians, relate the story of a gang of armed robbers whose fame had reached the ears of the court at that time. The first egg contains a little scene where a young girl is being attacked by the robbers in a forest and is saved by a valiant cavalry sergeant called Louis Gillet. And once open, the second egg reveals a scene in which the young girl is seen arriving at her house in the company of the handsome soldier. (This very popular theme was used elsewhere in France for the decoration of earthenware objects, notably by the well known Islettes factory, in eastern France. It was also the subject of many a melodrama at the beginning of the nineteenth century.)

In both cases, the bases of the eggs are in gilded wood and the supporting tripods in ordinary painted wood, decorated with stripes of gold leaf. At the level of the egg's supporting structure, each of the branches of the tripods is embellished with a bull's head in earthenware, the horns being made of copper wire. The cave which serves as a background for the first egg is made of fine clay, the tree is of earthenware, its foliage represented by tiny vegetable flowers. The mosses which cover the cave seem to be fragments of velvet material, likewise the hair of the figures, who are themselves in earthenware. The whole scene is supported by cardboard.

In the second egg the tiny house is made of painted cardboard and

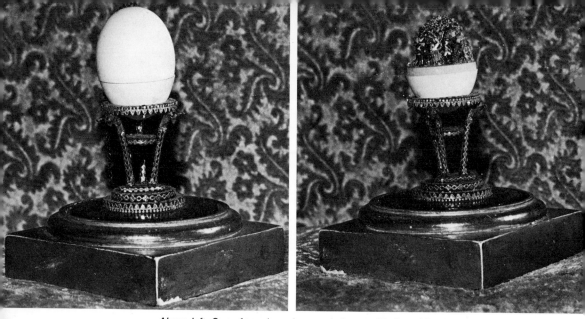

Above left: One of two 'surprise eggs' given to Madame Victoire, aunt of Louis XVI, Easter 1783. These eggs, which are externally similar, contain different scenes illustrating the kidnapping of a young girl and her rescue by a gallant soldier, an event which really occurred in France at that time.

Above right: The first egg open, on its original tripod. *Musée Lambinet, Versailles*

Left: The second egg open, on its original tripod. *Musée Lambinet, Versailles*

The rescue of the young girl from the highwaymen by a certain corporal Louis Gillet. *Musée Lambinet, Versailles*

the tiles on the roof are bands of painted paper. The leaves of the creeper at the back of the house have been cut out of a green silk material. Perhaps surprisingly, the author of those little masterpieces has always remained unknown.

These surprise eggs are of course small, a fact which may not be detected by looking at their photographs, since the height of the figures is only 6 mm and the cave itself for example is only 15 mm high. The house, which can look quite large on a photo, is about 26 mm high and 23 mm wide. In fact, the diameter of the eggs themselves is only 45 mm, not quite two inches.

It goes without saying that the members of the French royal family had adopted the habit of exchanging eggs at Easter, but they were not alone in this, as many other extravagant eggs were being made

31

The young girl arriving home after her ordeal. *Musée Lambinet, Versailles*

and exchanged during the second half of the eighteenth century in France. In Germany also the goldsmiths sometimes surpassed themselves. The enamelling workshops in the town of Augsburg were in advance of their French equivalents as far as the goldsmiths' work on Easter eggs was concerned, as their best period was between 1720 and 1750; and Augsburg Easter eggs, always enamelled and mounted on gold, are today very rare collectors' items.

Eggs of extraordinary magnificence were being produced in Paris, and it was probably these that inspired the great Russian goldsmith, Carl Fabergé, a century later. At the same time, Russian goldsmiths of the eighteenth century were themselves producing exceptional *objets d'art*, including an Easter egg in gold with a watch inside it, the work of Ivan Koulibine, made some time between 1765

and 1769. This watch-egg is today in the Hermitage Museum in Leningrad.

Another extraordinary creation of the eighteenth century goldsmiths is a 'surprise egg' in the collection of the Danish royal family in the palace of Rosenborg, in Copenhagen. According to family tradition, this egg, in ivory and gold, was made in Paris and offered to Queen Caroline of England, wife of George II – this explains the two letters 'c' engraved under a royal crown on the egg – by a Duchess Charlotte of Orleans. At first sight it looks like a very simple egg in ivory, hardly bigger than a normal hen's egg; but inside is another egg in gold slightly smaller, which in turn contains a chicken in gold with diamonds for eyes, a diamond ring and a tiny royal crown adorned with forty diamonds and six pearls (see illustration p. 100).

33

Easter egg in agate mounted on gold, probably made in England around 1760. *Cliché des Musées Nationaux, France*

Right: A beautiful Easter egg in tortoiseshell inlaid with mother of pearl and gold motifs, probably Italian from the middle of the 18th century. *Cliché des Musées Nationaux, France*

Many other equally magnificent eggs were made at the time, but one would need to be lucky indeed to come across any of them for sale. The Hermitage in Leningrad, for instance, possesses a Parisian egg of great beauty, made by an unknown French goldsmith for the Empress Elizabeth, whose monogram appears on the shell. It contains a gold *nécessaire* in gold and enamel adorned with one brilliant and several pink diamonds. Inside is a small watch.

The Louvre Museum, in Paris, also has in its keeping some remarkable Easter eggs which date from the same period. Among these is an egg in blood-red jasper enclosed in gold filigree in the Louis XV style, adorned with two diamonds and dating from about 1750. Another, supposed to be English, is in light-coloured agate mounted on gold. Its origin is, however, dubious. Equally suspect in pedigree is a porcelain egg mounted on gold, resembling an egg from Augsburg, which is also attributed to English manufacture by the

34

35

Another beautiful royal Easter egg from the castle of Versailles, an ostrich egg mounted on pomegranate wood and ivory. There is a legend that the ivory was turned by Madame Adelaide, aunt of Louis XVIII. The ostrich egg is decorated with a painting, by Lebel, of an assembly in a park. *Cliché des Musées Nationaux, France*

Above: One of a pair of royal Easter eggs from the last half of the 18th century and presently kept in the castle of Versailles. It is an ostrich egg mounted on boxwood and ebony, the tripod being ornamented with three ramsheads.

Louvre authorities. This must be a case of mistaken identity. And the great French museum has yet another Easter egg which is said to date from the middle of the eighteenth century and this time to be of Italian origin. Made from light-coloured shell, it is inlaid with mother-of-pearl and gold filaments representing people and flowers. Whatever their origins, however, all gold eighteenth-century Easter eggs are today very scarce collectors' pieces indeed. King Louis XVI continued the custom of giving and receiving eggs established at the court of France, but these became more sophisticated than the ostrich eggs presented by the Versailles zoo. The case is quoted of an Easter egg in gold covered in precious stones which he is said to have offered to a particularly beautiful *marquise* of the court. He abandoned the idea of giving natural dyed and decorated eggs at Easter, as his predecessors had done. Instead, he was the first of many monarchs to slip pearls and precious stones in eggs, which he offered at Easter to people he liked and whom he wished to help financially.

It was, therefore, in the eighteenth century that the Easter egg, the old pagan symbol, finally lost whatever symbolic value it had had, at least as far as the very rich were concerned. The Easter egg became a rich man's trinket and even a work of art. Then, after the French revolution, the fashion of offering beautifully made Easter eggs declined. The great revolutionaries, badly mistaken, thought that the eggs represented a uniquely Christian symbol. However, as might be guessed, the prohibition was completely ignored among the common people, and in all the villages of France, revolution or not, the custom of exchanging natural eggs continued unabated. Even in Paris artificial eggs containing miniature Bastilles were sold in large numbers.

After the degeneration of the revolution, Easter eggs once more experienced a revival, which reached even greater heights of enthusiasm under the Empire, when, for the first time, eggs were produced in alabaster (which is still an Italian speciality), as well as in ivory, wood and occasionally in porcelain.

The town of Dieppe, an important ivory production centre in the seventeenth and eighteenth centuries, produced some magnificent sculptured eggs. This centre, located on the sea, became extremely active under Louis XIII who visited Dieppe in 1617 and is said to

French mounted ostrich egg of the Empire period. The egg, supported by three little negro slaves in bronze, is placed on a gilt painted porcelain base. *Collection Friedman, Brussels*

have bought numerous ivory trinkets in the town. The most important objects produced in Dieppe were crucifixes, tobacco graters, statuettes on ebony bases and a variety of boxes and lockets. Thousands of ivory madonnas came out of the Dieppe workshops during this period. Under Louis XV and Louis XVI this small commerce lost its importance, but, even under these sovereigns, it never completely stopped. Even in 1760, there was still a well known shop in Dieppe specialising in ivory trinkets, that of the widow Ricoeur. It might have been possible to buy ivory Easter eggs there, similar to the one which the Dieppe museum keeps, a case in the form of an egg engraved with pastoral and courtly scenes such as were greatly in vogue during the eighteenth century.

The production of ivory eggs did not decline at the end of the eighteenth century as one might be led to believe. Eggs of this type were still being made in the nineteenth century, but, as they are unmarked, their places of origin will remain forever unknown.

Some beautiful enamel eggs were also produced in South Staffordshire at the end of the eighteenth century, but they were not Easter eggs as they were mainly employed as vinaigrettes, snuffboxes and even nutmeg graters.

Collectors may wish to know that beautiful enamel Easter eggs were being produced in 1977 by the firm Halcyon Days Enamels, of London. They are reminiscent of the eighteenth-century *objets d'art*. Made by Bilston craftsmen, the eggs are decorated with spring flowers framed by leaf-green rococo scrolls against a pink stippled background. Fortunately these charming eggs have been dated.

EUROPEAN EASTER CUSTOMS

For a variety of reasons, political and social, the ancient Easter customs which were more or less strictly observed for centuries everywhere in Europe have now largely lost their appeal, although the practice of exchanging eggs still survives, even in communist countries. Indeed, the practice seems so well buried in the minds of so many millions of people that it will probably continue forever. On the other hand, many of the associated Easter customs, the origins of which have also been lost in the past, are slowly dying. These customs, mainly of pagan origin and part of folklore rather than religion, are more often than not connected with ethnic or regional groups, though there are no strict social, cultural or even geographical lines of demarcation. One example, the custom of 'rolling' eggs down a slope or any inclined plane, is still practised in Scotland, Ireland, western England, France, Belgium, Rumania and Greece as well as in Russia. It is found in Poland in a slightly different guise: there, on Easter Sunday, the peasants dye their eggs, have them blessed by priests, and then roll them along the borders of their fields, hoping in so doing to protect the harvest from thunder— again, a ritual with more pagan than Christian association. At one time the same peasants used to rub eggs against the forehead of their sick animals to encourage a miraculous recovery.

The significance of 'rolling' eggs on Easter Sunday remains the same everywhere. It perhaps recalls the descent of the 'Angel of the Lord' from heaven who rolled back the stone from the door of the tomb of Christ.

A second custom which enjoys a curious international popularity is a game which is usually played on Easter Monday. Two boys with an egg in each hand try to crack them open by knocking them against each other. Mention of this strange practice is recorded in various documents dating back to the fourteenth century, and for centuries village boys have certainly been playing this game in Germany, Greece, Belgium, Ireland, Serbia, Macedonia and elsewhere. In the French province of Lorraine, boys used to play a game of bowls with the eggs, trying to crack them open. In the north of England, where the game is referred to as 'jarping', the participants must keep their right elbow stiffly pressed against their bodies, and each one must try to 'jarp', or crack the top of the other's egg.

The custom of egg-cracking may appear strange at first sight, but its significance soon becomes clear. By getting the eggs to break, people were unconsciously reconstructing the mystery of the creation of the world.

The Easter Meal

One custom which appears actually to have gained in popularity is that of eating a huge meal on Easter Sunday. This ceremony had great importance a long time ago, when people had to fast for forty days preceding Easter, but it is less understandable today when Lent is not very strictly kept, if at all. The tradition goes back at least to the Middle Ages, when 'egg-feasts' were organised on Easter Sunday practically everywhere. Rabelais, the great French writer of the sixteenth century, mentions in his books the monstrous Easter Sunday omelettes that people enjoyed in all the villages and towns of France. Special fairs were also organised: France had her 'blue egg fairs' and 'red egg fairs' in different parts of the country. In Poland, not so long ago, and in contemporary Greece, the women take baskets full of various foods to church on Easter Saturday, to get them blessed by the priest. The food is then duly eaten the following day.

In the past, in certain Polish and Bohemian villages, the priest himself used to go round the houses on Easter Saturday to bless the dining-room tables and all that stood on them. Poland, like present-day Bohemia, still observes a very ancient custom in which diners, before being allowed to eat, have to share pieces of hard-boiled eggs and wish each other the best of luck. This being properly done, the participants then sit down and consume huge meals, followed by traditional pastries such as *mazureks* and *babkas*, to the accompaniment of quantities of vodka. A long time ago, the entire Polish nation would wait impatiently for the coming of Easter and the end of Lent.

Members of the ancient Polish guilds who took part in processions organised on Palm Sunday would sing:

'– Jesus is coming
He will take the soup and the herrings
He will leave us the dry sausages and will bless . . .'

In Holy Russia, the Easter dinner was a long and well observed tradition. This is still the custom even today, and few old Russians would miss an Easter meal with all the family attending; a dinner which includes the traditional Russian Easter pastries, the *koulitch* or the *paskas*, small peculiarly Russian cheese cakes which are only made during the Holy Week.

The tradition of the Easter meal, which is shared by Catholics, Protestants, the Orthodox churches and the Jews, recalls, according to certain historians, the last meal of Christ, the Lord's Supper, though this is obviously disputable. It seems more likely to have been a kind of collective relief of tension after the forty days of fast.

The pre-Easter Purifications

In practically all countries, the gift of eggs was often preceded by a curious, pagan-inspired, ritual of purification. This is held during Holy Week, but in some isolated cases, on Easter Monday. First of all the homes had to be cleaned from top to bottom, a task which is still called 'spring cleaning' in Britain. Until recently, in all the villages of Europe, householders were kept busy whitewashing their houses, painting the woodwork, papering the walls, giving the garden a trim, cutting the hedges – and often buying new clothes. In Iran today, where the New Year falls on the spring equinox, the festival is called the 'feast of the new clothes'.

The custom of buying new clothes is so well established that it is still observed in the villages and small towns of Russia, Poland, France, Germany, Hungary, Czechoslovakia, Greece, Rumania and elsewhere. As with every other Easter tradition, people are unconsciously following an ancestral urge: the buying of new clothes is an act of purification and renewal.

In many places in Europe there are remnants of other less obvious rituals of purification, some of them involving strange 'magical' rites which must have a definite pagan origin. In Czechoslovakia, for instance, the ritual starts on the Wednesday preceding Easter, the 'sad Wednesday', when people are engaged in cleaning their houses. Then, on Good Friday, before the break of dawn, the young peasant girls go down to wash themselves in nearby rivulets, which act is supposed to ensure their future good health and beauty. In Poland the young girls also wash themselves in a stream, but they do it on Maundy Thursday, and this is supposed to make them 'as red as blood, as white as snow, as healthy as a nut and as attractive as an apple' for a whole year. This tradition which is also observed in Hungary, demands that the girls carry out the ceremony in secret, though no one knows why.

In Poland, one other custom which has been passed down the centuries seems to have its roots in a form of purification. It is the *dyngus*, of definite pagan origin like the others, but limited to Central Europe. On Easter Monday, young girls and young men soak themselves with water amidst much laughter and amusement. It is a kind of water fight, where the main tactics consist in securing the water supplies. The Polish boys may soak the girls only on Easter Monday, but the girls have the privilege of being allowed to attack the boys any time until Whitsunday. The rite is even more conspicuous in Hungary where the young men, also on Easter Monday, visit houses where girls of marrying age live. Once the door is open the boy says 'Good day, good day, my lily, I water you to keep you from withering'. Then the young girl comes out, in her most beautiful traditional dress, and once outside she is sprayed with a little water. She then gives the boy a present of dyed or decorated eggs.

Most of these customs have all but disappeared nowadays, but the old Poles and Hungarians still spray some perfume on the ladies on Easter Monday, an example followed by many a young modern boy. After all, it is only the gesture that matters. In the act of 'watering' the young girl is clearly establishing a link with some antique fertility rite.

A water game once played by the clergymen of France, despite a church ban during the fifteenth century, should also be mentioned here. This was the *jeu des paresseux* (the game of the lazy ones), when clergymen known for their 'laziness' were taken forcibly to the church, with only a shirt on, and, once in the church, were drenched with water by their colleagues.

Other customs involving purification are recorded all over Europe. Documents dating from the darkest Middle Ages mention that in Brittany, on Easter Sunday, the fishmongers were thrown into the water – as a reprisal for having gorged the people with fish during the forty days of fasting! But most of these customs, which might seem simply harmless pastimes, were in fact condemned at one time or another by the church.

In England, right up until the end of the seventeenth century, the king and queen, on Maundy Thursday, washed the feet of twelve old men, in memory of the apostles. William III was the first sovereign to refuse to do this himself, instructing his chaplain to stand in for him. A Frenchman, Colsoni, in his *Guide de l'ètranger à Londres* published in 1693, states that: 'On Maundy Thursday, the king, following a very ancient custom, washes the feet of as many old men as he has years of age and the queen the feet of as many old women as she has years of age'.

The Easter floggings
Many acts of flagellation at Easter are recorded in various countries, such as Poland, Czechoslovakia and France, but once again the church attempted to put a halt to the practice in the Middle Ages, although it is still seen in Easter processions in certain parts of Spain. The custom recalls the flagellation of Christ and does not seem to have a pagan origin like so many others. At one time it was a very popular custom and it is known that at the old Emmaus Fair in Krakov at Easter, they went as far as selling rods for flagellation. In the province of Jura, in France, churchgoers came down from the hills 'to seek a pardon' in the valley church, beating each other very convincingly all the way down. A survival of the custom still exists in Czechoslovakia where the young men, on Easter Monday, go from house to house armed with willow rods, and asking for presents, *na koledu*, mainly where young women of marrying age live. They beat the girls very gently and in return the girls give the boys some *kraslice*, the traditional decorated Easter eggs of the country. The intention here is not very clear, for the act does not seem to recall the flagellation of Christ at all.

Palm Sunday customs

Ever since the Middle Ages, on Palm Sunday (sometimes called Hosannah Sunday) faithful parishioners, if they are lucky enough to live in Mediterranean countries such as Italy or Spain, take palms to church – if they live in the colder regions they use instead branches of rosemary, of laurel or of myrtle. In Western Europe, where palmtrees are few and far between, boxwood has always been a favourite, and up to the nineteenth century, all rosaries and Easter eggs were made out of that wood. In Central and Eastern Europe, including Russia, branches of willow were used, bearing white or yellow buds, depending upon whether Easter was early or late in the season. Willow trees, like the oaks, have however been slowly disappearing from European countrysides and in Germany they have actually been replaced at Easter with artificial branches in plastic, on which are hung plastic eggs!

The connection between the green branches and ancient fertility beliefs is clear in many of these old practices. In Czechoslovakia, for instance, on the day preceding Palm Sunday, the men from the villages went down to the valleys to cut branches from the willows which line the numerous rivulets. The branches were then cleaned and planted in the fields to make sure that the year's harvest would be good. In other countries, such as France and Belgium, branches of boxwood, once they had been blessed by the priest, were placed in the house, usually above the entrance door, by the photograph of a deceased member of the family or attached to the crucifix. These rituals no doubt represented a very un-Christian means of protecting the house and its inhabitants against any spell which might be cast upon them! Boxwood talismans were also put in the stables to protect the animals. In certain Mediterranean regions, such as in Provence and in Spain, and also in Flanders, a branch was placed in the hands of the dead. In Poland, while it was the willow branches that possessed the magical powers of protection, palms were painted on houses during spring cleaning in order to inform passers-by that a young girl of marrying age lived there.

The blessing of branches on Palm Sunday is of ancient origin, and most historians believe that it recalls the palms waved at Christ when he made his entry into Jerusalem. It seems that in the fourth century AD, Saint Cyrillus, Bishop of Jerusalem, told his flock that the palm tree from which the branches were taken to welcome Christ into the city still existed in the Kidron valley. Whether this was true or not, the custom was adopted very early by all the churches of the East and in the Egyptian monasteries.

But that the ritual recalls only the entry into Jerusalem is not convincing, if one considers the many uses to which palms have been put in the past and the many beliefs which have been attached to them, such as that they have powers of protection against thunder, and evil spells. It seems that the roots of these practices are much older, and go back to some unidentified pagan ritual, taken over by the Christian church.

The waving of palms by the exultant crowds watching the arrival of Christ may of course be only a transposition, by the writers of the New Testament, of the *adventus*, the welcoming of a victorious Roman emperor to Rome. But it is true that for centuries, at least since the fourteenth century, the entry into Jerusalem has been reenacted in many regions. In south Germany, in Austria, in Switzerland, the local bishop did not hesitate to take the place of Christ in the procession, mounted first on a real donkey, then on an artificial donkey made of wood, the famous *palmesel* of the Germans. Many of these *palmesels* are to be seen in museums in Germany and Switzerland.

The reformists put an end to this Easter Sunday carnival and the 'Easter donkeys' were taken away from the churches, the Zurich one being thrown into the lake in 1521. Customs are hard to eradicate, though, and *palmesels* were used in Austria until the second half of the eighteenth century when the Emperor Joseph II took stern measures to put an end to their use.

Right: A German 'palmesel' (Easter donkey) from the Middle Ages, such as was carried during the Palm Sunday procession. This one dates from 1380 and is in the Germanisches Nationalmuseum of Nuremburg.

THE EGGS IN THE EASTER CUSTOMS

Easter customs are so varied and numerous that it is practically impossible to record them all, for they differ from region to region, from village to village. They are all, up to a certain point, of pagan origin. For instance, the ceremony of the 'first steps', to mention only one, which took place in Provence, is almost completely pagan in character. During the week preceding Easter, parents tried to make their babies walk while the church bells were ringing the *Gloria*. This was intended to keep the babies immune from being affected with gallstones during their lifetimes.

As for the strange uses to which Easter eggs were put, these leave no doubt as to their magical implications. Spanish chronicles of the fifteenth century, for instance, tell the story of how Margaret, who had been for a little while the wife of Don Juan, son of Isabella the Catholic, went on pilgrimage to Brou cathedral in Bresse, in France. There she witnessed a rather strange ceremony. Young couples could be seen dancing on the church square which was littered with great quantities of eggs. All those couples who managed to finish the dance without having broken an egg could then get married without parental interference: permission could not be denied. While the Infanta Margaret was watching the ceremony, a beautiful young man riding a white horse arrived. He was the Prince of Savoy. The Infanta and the Prince then danced in the square and did not break any eggs. They were married the following Easter, and ever after, state the chronicles, the couple offered beautiful artificial eggs full of sweets to their relatives and friends at Easter time. This is, in fact, the only reference to artificial eggs in any western document as early as the fifteenth century.

On the other side of Europe, in Serbia, on Easter Sunday the peasants buried red eggs in their vineyards in the hope of a rich harvest the following autumn. And in Macedonia, eggs were buried

Russian enamel egg.

18th-century ivory Easter egg. *Dieppe Museum, France*

Enamel egg (Chinese).

Dyed and decorated eggs from Czechoslovakia. *Czech Tourist Office*

Dyed and decorated natural eggs from Romania.

Russian wooden nest-egg, completely dismantled to show that it is composed of six different eggs which can be fitted inside each other.

Russian wooden *pissankis*.

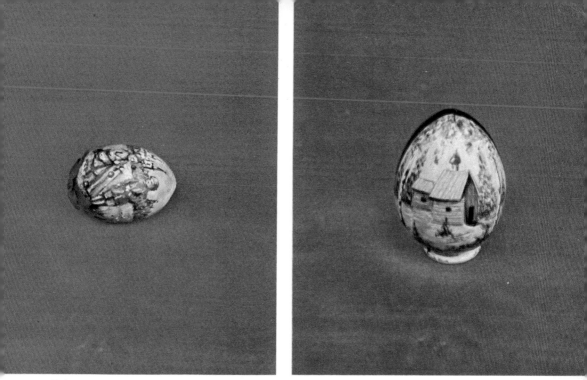

Two Russian papier-mâché eggs, probably made in the United States for the Russian community.

Large Russian porcelain egg painted with the monogram of Tsar Nicholas II.
Collection Deprins

Very elegant porcelain egg mounted on bronze, from the end of the 19th century. Probably Berlin, but unmarked.

A 19th-century carved ivory Easter egg. *Collection Wery*

Six novelty eggs in porcelain.

An English Easter egg in the shape of a bonbonnière, manufactured by Hammersleys, of Longton, Staffordshire.

An extraordinary German porcelain Easter egg from the beginning of the 19th century, showing the goddess of spring and a fawn standing against the upright and decapitated egg. The pedestal is painted with the word *'Ostara'*. It is one of the first examples of a modern pagan Easter egg.

at each corner of the field to protect the grapes from hail and thunder, the two main enemies of the vineyards. In Rumania there still exists another custom, which is also recorded in Russia. On Maundy Thursday, the village children, as they do in many other places, go from house to house collecting eggs, in exchange for which they give tiny green branches. The eggs are then dyed, painted or decorated during the two following days, and before dawn on Easter Sunday, the children take them to the cemeteries. There they present them, together with small loaves of bread, to the poorest of the village. The branches given by the children in exchange for the eggs are in turn set on fire in the courtyards or gardens of each home, as a means of winning protection from evil spirits.

There are many legends connected with the Easter egg custom that are still told to young children today. One concerns the pilgrimage of the church bells to Rome. As the bells remain silent between Good Friday and Easter Sunday, the children are told that they have 'gone to Rome to fetch the Easter eggs'. And when they are heard again on Easter Sunday, the children run out into the gardens and collect the eggs, none ever admitting that he has seen his parents doing the bells' work.

Another legend, of definite German origin, is that of the Easter hare. The story, born in southern Germany, spread to neighbouring regions, passed into Alsace, then to France and other European countries, where the hares became rabbits. In Alsace parents still explain very seriously that 'the red Easter eggs are brought by the white hares', which explains why the hare is very often associated with the Easter iconography. What is the source of the legend? Nobody knows for sure, but it is possible to postulate that, a long time ago, villagers noticed that the hare brings forth his young very early in the season. And baby rabbits roam the countryside even before Easter. The hare story could thus be another remnant of a long forgotten fertility rite.

DYED AND DECORATED EGGS

The first dyed eggs appeared on a wide scale in Europe some time in the thirteenth century. These eggs were dyed red, and they were followed by eggs dyed in other colours such as blue, mauve, green or yellow, depending no doubt on the vegetable dyes available in the region where they were produced. This remarkable, unconcerted but international innovation reached practically all countries including France, the Low Countries, Germany, Italy, Spain and the Eastern European countries – in fact from the Atlantic shores to the Urals.

The first question that arises is: why were the first eggs of this type dyed red? This is a very controversial question. Certain Christian historians claim that red was chosen because it recalls the blood of the Passion of Christ; while other scholars point out that red symbolises light and fire, two of the four elements necessary to maintain life.

There are many legends connected with the red Easter egg, and the best known among them was started by the Roman historian Lamprinus. According to this respected writer, the day that Emperor Marcus Aurelius Severus was born, in 208 AD, one of his mother's hens laid an egg covered with red spots. This unusual egg was duly taken to be examined by a diviner, who declared that the red spots were a sign that the new-born boy would one day become emperor of Rome. The mother kept the prediction a secret until 224 AD, when Marcus Aurelius was proclaimed emperor, as the diviner had predicted. As might be guessed, the Romans then took to offering eggs dyed in different colours to each other as good luck talismans. The Christians took over the well established Roman custom by simply diverting the symbol to suit their own needs. By exchanging eggs at Easter, the Christians were perhaps wishing each other progress towards the spiritual kingdom.

In Russia, red eggs were offered in memory of the red egg supposed to have been offered by Mary Magdalene to Christ, after the resurrection, a belief which is not of course corroborated by the Gospel.

Whatever the truth of these accounts, the dyed egg has remained supreme for centuries throughout Europe and elsewhere. In Iran, for instance, the New Year, which falls at Easter time, is still called 'the feast of the red egg'. And in Romania, a well known proverb states that 'when the Christians stop dyeing their eggs red, the end of the world will be approaching'. In Greece, Maundy Thursday is called 'Red Thursday' because it is on that particular day that the eggs are

Two postcards illustrating Easter legends: 1. the church-bells going to Rome (1912); 2. the hares who bring the Easter eggs (1904).

51

dyed, and a genuine Easter egg could never be anything but red. In Czechoslovakia, where Easter has always been celebrated with much fervour, the word *kraslice*, which means 'beautiful egg', is mentioned in documents dating from the thirteenth century, when the word in fact referred to the red colour of the egg – the original meaning was afterwards lost and its concept mingled with the word *krassa*, which means 'beauty'. And, in Bohemia, the celebrations of Easter are called 'the red feasts'.

As in Czechoslovakia, the words 'beauty' and 'red' are also confounded in the Russian language, and linguists cannot agree on whether the famous Moscow square was red or whether it was beautiful. Exactly the same happens in the Hungarian language, in which the concepts 'red' and 'Easter' are encapsulated in one word, *kokonya*.

Not so long ago, in Bulgaria, on Easter Sunday, a red egg was hidden in a huge cake and the youngest member of the family was blind folded and expected to find it, and distribute pieces of it to the other members present saying, as he went along: 'Little egg red with the blood of Christ, give him (or her) life and health'.

For whatever reason, then, the colour red remained dominant in

Natural dyed and decorated Easter eggs from Czechoslovakia.

Easter folklore. But the villagers were soon to discover that they could dye their eggs other colours by using vegetable dyes. These they could produce very cheaply by boiling various natural substances. To get yellow eggs, they simply had to drop them for a few seconds in a dye prepared with onion peels. To obtain a redder colour, the eggs were left in the water a little longer, or placed in a dye prepared with beet juice. Brown eggs were easily made by dipping them in boiling tea or coffee, or in a dye prepared from oak bark or alder bark. To get beautiful green eggs, nothing could beat a dye made out of spinach leaves or nettle roots. Blue eggs were made with dyes prepared from mallow or logwood.

It should be added here that at a later date, chemical dyes were also used, which offered an even greater variety of colours. But, whatever the dye used, a few drops of concentrated vinegar was always added to the water to obtain more vivid tones. In general the eggs were hardboiled, for more than an hour sometimes, to make them so hard that they could be kept for years. In certain cases, before the dyeing operation, the eggs were emptied by piercing a hole at each extremity with a needle and sucking out the contents; then the two tiny holes were filled with wax. But whether empty or hardboiled, once the eggs were dyed, they were left to dry thoroughly and then rubbed very gently with oil to add lustre and protect the colour.

At an uncertain period of our history, but at least as early as the Middle Ages, people rediscovered the ancient practice of decorating their eggs rather more elaborately. With a few strokes of paint, you could give the egg a face. You could just as easily write on the shells the names of the people who were to receive them. Slowly, various decorative techniques were developed, mainly in Eastern and Central Europe. And those techniques soon became standardised throughout that region, an unbelievable but true development, and one that has not changed for countless generations. Egg decorating rapidly became a genuine popular art, and from Bulgaria to Poland, from Czechoslovakia to the eastern borders of Russia, it still flourishes. In Western Europe, however, the decoration of eggs, apart from dyeing them, has never been more than an occasional affair. One can only conclude that the common inspiration is of Slavic origin.

Artists at the Kalocsa handicraft centre, Hungary, painting Easter eggs.

Unless one is a trained egg specialist, it is practically impossible to differentiate between a Bulgarian egg and a Polish egg, or between a Hungarian one and a Polish one, except in a few specific cases. Dyed or decorated eggs have also received special names in various languages. They are called *pissankis* in Russia, *pisankis* in Polish, *kraslices* in Czech, *pâquelets* in France and *cocognes* in Belgium.

The first decorating technique, the simplest one in fact, is that known as 'batik', from the Hungarian *batik*, an ancient method used to dye fabric. The general principle of the method is to dip a pen, a goose quill, a pin, or even a *tjantung* (a special instrument used in the textile industry of Hungary), in melted wax and to trace designs with it on the surface of the eggs, which are then placed in a lukewarm dye bath – lukewarm to prevent the wax from melting. When the desired shade is reached, it remains only to remove the egg, to let it dry thoroughly and to take the wax off, revealing the designs dyed on the shell.

When an egg is to be painted in several colours, the wax is left on the shell after the first bath, and further designs are drawn on it. The shell is then placed in a second dye bath. The operation can be repeated three, four or five times to obtain eggs decorated with three, four or five different colours. Wax is the most usual material used, though it is not the only one. In Czechoslovakia, for example, people use sauerkraut juice. Some use lemon juice and even plain vinegar.

Another way of decorating eggs is by an etching technique. Here, various motifs are drawn on the shell, already dyed, with a pen dipped in hydrochloric acid. The acid bites into the colour and removes it, leaving a decorative design behind. The egg is then carefully washed in cold water, dried and rubbed with oil.

A further means of obtaining similar results is to adopt the scratching technique, where a design is scratched on to the dyed egg by means of a sharp instrument. However, this technique requires a very steady hand.

Painted egg from Romania (yellow, red, dark brown).

Natural dyed and decorated eggs from Bulgaria. *Permission of Ethnographic Museum, Sofia, Bulgaria*

56

Four Czech dyed and
decorated eggs.

Hungarian Easter eggs.

A fourth technique, which gives very pleasant results, is practised in most countries of Eastern Europe, and has often been called 'the blocking technique'. Leaves or flowers are dipped in oil or even in the white of an egg, then arranged around a hardboiled egg. The egg is then wrapped in a piece of gauze and dipped in a dye bath. When completely dry, the gauze and the pieces of plants are carefully removed, leaving their imprints on the shell.

The fifth technique, known as the 'appliqué' method, is very much in favour in Moravia and in Poland, mainly in the region of Bialystok. In Poland, a marrow-like substance obtained from rushes is applied to the dyed or natural-coloured shells. But in Moravia, bits of yellow straw are soaked for half an hour in water to make them soft. The straw is then cut into various shapes, mainly triangles, squares, stripes and diamonds. These are dyed, then glued on the shells. Eggs decorated in this manner by the Moravians may

58

be covered with between one hundred and three hundred pieces of straw.

Other eggs are painted with water colour or oil paint, the eggs being mostly hardboiled beforehand. Probably the finest eggs of this elegant type come from the region of Kalocsa, in Hungary. Most of these glorious and bright Hungarian Easter eggs are decorated with floral motifs, such as tulips or carnations, set off by scrolls and crowns.

Elsewhere, too, the motifs are borrowed from nature, and flowers are very popular for instance in Russia and in Bulgaria. Hundreds of other motifs have been used to decorate these fragile Easter eggs, quite apart from linear and geometrical figures. Zoomorphic and anthropomorphic figures are found everywhere. In Bulgaria, eggs are found decorated with grapes, vineleaves, branches, roses, geraniums, violets, pine trees, pears, apples, cherries, as well as bees, spiders, chicks, roosters and fishes. In certain regions of Czechoslovakia, one finds eggs decorated with stylised flowers, a variety of animals including horses, wild sheep and roosters, and very often shepherd heads. Such figures tend to conform to certain well-defined forms and conventions.

The natural and wooden decorated Easter eggs of the republic of the Ukraine, where they have been painted for God knows how many centuries, deserve detailed treatment, for the ancient custom of exchanging eggs at Eastertide has perhaps been more meticulously observed there than anywhere else in Europe: particularly in the region of Poltava, in Bukovina and in Transcarpatia. Even today, painted eggs are still appreciated gifts in that part of the world;

Hungarian Easter eggs.

Painted egg from Czechoslovakia. (Yellow, red, brown.)

young men offer them to young girls and young girls offer them to young boys, as courtship presents; adults exchange Easter eggs as a sign of reconciliation and good will; and children receive them as toys. The old custom has been so well kept in the Ukraine that, even today, the nicest eggs received at Easter are carefully kept in the home through the year – up to the First World War, they were hung under the icons, on the whitewashed walls. Even modern interiors are decorated with colourful eggs.

But there is more to the tradition than decoration. For centuries colouring Easter Eggs has been a lively popular art all over the republic. Every town and village takes a pride in local mastery of techniques handed down through centuries. Indeed the ancestors of the Ukrainian people were already producing Easter eggs in ceramic between the tenth and thirteenth centuries, some of which can still be seen in Ukrainian museums.

Ukrainian eggs are characteristically ornamented with designs which date back to the ancient Tripolie culture of neolithic times. For instance the 'Ukrainian meander' is a discontinuous wavy motif found on eggs produced in Volhynia, Podolia, in North Bukovina, in Transcarpatia and in the regions of Poldava and Kherson. Other designs are based on a solar motif, which appears in various forms.

The eggs from Galicia, for instance, often display rather stylised suns, like very simple round medallions, though they are representations of the sun nevertheless. On the other hand, the eggs from western Podolia are painted with realistic and recognisable springtime suns.

Polish Easter eggs decorated in a technique practised only in Poland and Czechoslovakia: the eggs are covered with a marrow-like substance obtained from rushes. *Polish Interpress Agency*

Among other favourite Ukrainian subjects, equally transmitted from generation to generation, is the strange image of the 'goddess', which could be Mokoch, Bereguina or Jiva, once more indicating the pagan symbolism still alive in the Easter egg. Yet other designs are geometrical, for instance the 'chest' or the various shapes of 'wine containers', always very formalised, but recognisable. In fact it is almost impossible to list all the numerous Ukrainian designs, as nearly every village has its own, usually the same pattern as that used in local embroidery work. Like other East European peoples the Ukrainians have a special love for plant motifs, and one often finds eggs decorated with leaves, branches or flowers painted in a very free style. And some regions specialise in animal representations, as they have from the earliest times: eggs from the village of Kosmatch for instance, often have a 'running deer' or 'horse' on them, with antlers and manes always out of proportion. The Kosmatch eggs incidentally are the most sought after in the whole republic, followed by those from the villages of Stary Kossov and Verbovetz. Those eggs are completely different in turn from those produced in the Goutsoule region of the central Ukraine, which are of very special interest because they are sometimes so delicate as to be reminiscent of Indian, Chinese or Japanese miniatures. A very ancient legend of the Goutsoule region tells how once upon a time lived a monster, Pecoune, far beyond high mountains and dangerous rivers. This enemy of mankind was waiting for the end of the world and used to send out scouts to see whether men were still living in peace and observing the practice of exchanging eggs. He rejoiced every time he was told that there was discord in the world, and he became very angry every time he learned that everything was in order, that villagers were happy and were still decorating eggs. For he knew that the world would continue to flourish as long as its inhabitants kept decorating Easter eggs, and that it would disappear the day the people abandoned the ancient custom.

At the end of the nineteenth century, following a trend throughout Europe, the Ukrainians began to produce – and are still producing – wooden Easter eggs, beautifully hand painted by master craftsmen in the numerous handicraft workshops of the republic, notably in Transcarpatia, in Bukovina and in the two regions of Poldava and Kherson. Those workshops, which are now encouraged by the state, produce countless wooden souvenirs to be sold all over Russia as well as the wooden Easter eggs. The main producing centres, where one might expect to find the most beautiful wooden eggs, are at present in Lvov, in Kossov, in Ivano-Frankovsk, in Kolomya and of course in Kiev, the capital of the Ukraine.

Not all Ukrainian eggs of course are works of art, for every region of the republic also produces Easter eggs of a much simpler nature, decorated with colourful stripes and triangles or uneven blobs of paint.

Probably due to their fragility, natural Easter eggs from Central and Eastern European countries are rarely found outside their regions of origin, but one can hope to get hold of some of them, at Easter time, in the shops that several East European countries have established in Western capitals.

Right: Egg from Poland decorated with pith and coloured wool.

DECORATED WOODEN EGGS

About a hundred years ago, hand-decorated natural eggs were being replaced everywhere by machine-turned wooden eggs, painted with gouache or oil paint. These artificial eggs, which were representations of real hen's eggs, retained the names which had been given to the natural eggs, and they are still called *pissankis* in Russia or *pisankis* in Poland. When they first appeared they were thought too elegant to give to children, but towards the end of the nineteenth century it became customary to give them away as toys at Easter time. Such unbreakable eggs appeared in Russia, Poland and in Bulgaria at about the same time as the famous *matriochka*, the Russian nest-doll so popular with children. This originated in Zagorsk, near Moscow, but was soon being made in Semionov, near Gorki, in Kirov and Kalinine.

The wooden eggs of Russia, Poland, the Ukraine, Czechoslovakia, Hungary and Romania are very often painted by gifted artists, working in semi-official handicraft centres. The wooden Easter eggs made in the Ukraine, already described, are of especial beauty. In most countries of the West, the production of wooden eggs has long been abandoned, the costs being too high to make it profitable, but in Eastern Europe it is part of the folk art tradition. New examples are continually being made and new ornamental techniques developed.

Russia is renowned for its beautifully decorated wooden *pissankis* in plain wood, but less well known is the egg whose top can be unscrewed to reveal inside a small yellow chick. The Russians also produce sets of nesting eggs of diminishing sizes, all painted in different colours. Most of the wooden *pissankis* one finds outside Russia are produced by the handicrafts centres of Semyonov, near Gorki, or by the Gutsulshchina Handicrafts Association, in Kosov in the Ukraine. They can be obtained through the V/O 'Vneshposyl-

Russian enamel egg by Paul Ovtchinnikov. This egg can be unscrewed and the parts reassembled to form two egg cups. *Collection Poliakov*

A beautiful Russian Easter necklace. *Collection Deprins*

Russian 'necklace eggs'.

Russian egg, one picture showing the egg closed, engraved with the phrase
'*Kristos Voskresy*' (Christ is risen), the other showing the same egg opened to reveal a
hand-painted icon inside. This type of egg was very popular, and even Carl Fabergé
produced more than one. St Petersburg, end of 19th century.

A beautiful Easter egg in *pâte de verre*.

Miniature porcelain egg containing a tiny 'frozen Charlotte' doll. These eggs were not in fact genuine Easter eggs, but were given to the mothers of new-born babies.

Czech glass Easter egg of the Mary Gregory type. These eggs are now very scarce.
Probably Jablonec, end of 19th century.

Two rather attractive glass eggs. 'Paperweight' eggs have always been popular in Italy,
where they are still being made every year. The other egg, in blue crystal, is quite rare. It
was made by the Val St-Lambert manufacture in Belgium at the end of the 19th
century.

Two novelty Art Deco eggs in porcelain.

Miniature wooden egg, hand-painted and containing a tiny rosary. This type of egg, which dates from the end of the 19th century, was given to little girls on Easter Sunday.

Metal egg containing a thimble, threads and needles, a type which was very popular in Victorian times.

Fragile but elegant cardboard Easter egg covered with kid and painted by hand with an 18th-century scene. French, end of 19th century.

French cardboard Easter egg covered with printed silk.

torg', 32–34 Smolenskaya-Sennaya Square, Moscow G-200, USSR.

The Bavarians manufacture wooden eggs, painted in imitation marble of various shades.

It is sad to have to admit that in a world where profit is the ultimate criterion, the production of such lovely trinkets is probably already doomed. Opaque or transparent plastic Easter eggs, produced in Germany, Poland and Czechoslovakia, are even now making a gradual but significant appearance. This development will spell the end of the beautiful *pissankis* and *kraslices* in wood, still lovingly hand-painted by conscientious artists. In a few years it will be practically impossible to assemble a decent collection of them at a price ordinary people can afford.

RUSSIAN EASTER EGGS IN PAPIER-MACHÉ

It was towards the end of the eighteenth century that the transformation of the Easter egg into a trinket or a work of art began, and it was probably in France, or to be more accurate in Paris, that the movement, like so many eighteenth-century fashions, started. It was to reach its height however, in Russia, a hundred years later.

Like so many other countries, Russia had for centuries produced natural Easter eggs, but the practise of making artificial eggs did not appear until the end of the eighteenth century. First, Russian goldsmiths produced some striking examples of jewelled eggs; then the porcelain manufacturers began to make eggs, followed by the woodworkers, and then the glassmakers. But it was the beautifully varnished papier-maché Easter eggs which finally brought the art to its consummation.

If Russia under the Tsars produced eggs which are now sought after the world over, it is in no small measure due to an artistic movement which developed during the opening years of the nineteenth century. In reaction to the fashion for faithful imitation of Western art, certain Russian artists began to revive the art and folklore of Holy Russia, a few years after the great wars of the French empire. The pan-Slavic movement which based its ideology on a return to an art form essentially Russian and traditional, began under the reign of Tsar Nicholas 1 (1825–1855). The artists found their inspiration notably in a marvellous book by J. Georgi, *Description of the races of the Russian Empire*, translated into Russian from the German in 1776 and profusely illustrated with engravings.

Using these prints as models, porcelain makers began to make the now famous statuettes of groups of people wearing traditional dress. This immense break with the past and its academic rigidity, this rejection of the redundant romanticism of the west, reached a crisis on 9 November 1863, when thirteen artists led by the painter Kramskoi refused flatly to accept the compulsory subject set by the Moscow Academy, 'Odin in Walhalla'. The rebellion of these artists led to the foundation of 'The Wanderers', a free association of painters who saw themselves as united by a complete disregard of academic education and the stilted ideas of the past. This movement came radically to influence not only Russian painting, but also all other artistic fields, including that of the simple Easter egg.

According to the leaders of the dissident group, every work of art should serve both to teach and to denounce: in this case, to denounce the bourgeois and effete lifestyles of the rich and the powerful. What mattered was not necessarily the form nor the deep significance of the work, but the subject, its anecdotal quality and its inherent morality. This conception, simplistic as it no doubt was, acted as a kind of focal point for a new-born nationalism: it gave birth to a new Russian style.

The pan-Slavic movement was active in Russia until the 1917 revolution. Its effects spread to every form of art and heavily influenced the decorators of Easter eggs. The movement's doctrines deeply affected young painters, porcelain-modellers and decorators, nearly all the goldsmiths (with the exception of the most famous of them all, Carl Fabergé himself) and, as might be guessed, the craftsmen in papier-mâché.

Papier-mâché is a great Russian speciality. Even today most people are familiar with the admirable examples of highly polished papier-mâché ornaments of contemporary design, produced by some of the Russian handicraft centres where the art of the miniature is still kept alive. The most important of those centres is, without doubt, the ancient Russian village of Palekh, located a good hour's drive by car from the textile town of Ivanovo. Palekh has been renowned since the eighteenth century for its icon works. Today's craftsmen who live and work in Palekh still produce papier-mâché *objets d'art*, decorated with beautiful and fine miniatures illustrating historic events of the past, old Russian fairy tales, characters taken from classical Russian literature, *troikas* and songs.

Thirty kilometres from Palekh is another village called Kholoui, also a well-known craft centre, where papier-mâché objects are made, mainly boxes, in a style somewhat less elaborate than that of

Palekh. The village of Kholoui stretches out on both banks of the river Teza, a tributary of the Kliazma. As far back as the sixteenth century, Kholoui has been a great centre for the production of icons and embroideries, and it prides itself on having nurtured such famous icon painters as Lavroutchka Ivanov and Ivachka Pourilov, both active during the seventeenth century and both of whose descendants are still at work in Kholoui. While Palekh used to produce icons for the rich, Kholoui produced inexpensive works sold for a few kopeks in the country fairs of Russia. In 1668 it was stated in a charter signed by Tsar Alexei Mikhailovitch that in a 'certain village of the Souzdal district, called Kholoui, the villagers paint holy icons without either reflection or respect, with negligence and in an improper way'.

Regardless of this judgment, the incorrigible painters of Kholoui went on recreating religious scenes, however sacred, in the most realistic manner, using ultra-bright colours, mainly yellow and red, so that their icons came to be known in Russia as 'reddies'. In 1884, to revive the art of icon-painting, a school of painting was created in Kholoui under the supervision of the St Petersburg Academy of Arts. The school also educated wood carvers and gilders, for like their neighbours in Palekh, the people of Kholoui had started to make papier-mâché objects.

Both centres were producing papier-mâché Easter eggs by the end of the nineteenth century. The 1917 revolution brought a halt to the production of icons, so Palekh and Kholoui turned their energies to the production of papier-mâché boxes.

But of all the old papier-mâché production centres, no name is more famous than that of the village of Fedoskino, situated some thirty kilometres from Moscow, where the most beautiful papier-mâché Easter eggs ever conceived were produced late in the nineteenth century and at the beginning of the twentieth.

The village stands within the meanderings of the Outcha river, and its setting of verdant meadows and groves of birch trees makes it look like the scene of a Russian fairy tale. Little remains of the ancient Fedoskino except for a few *izbas* and an old well. Today, in the middle of the village stands the modern building housing 'the factory of miniatures' where about 350 people, inhabitants of Fedoskino and surrounding villages, are employed.

The papier-maché is still prepared exactly as it was in the old days. The paper and the cardboard are coated with glue, pressed, soaked in linseed oil, dried and redried, covered with mastic, painted with black lacquer on the outside, red lacquer on the inside and then varnished again, until the surface is perfectly flat and shiny. The resultant substance often has a resilience greater than that of real wood. The papier-maché is usually turned into boxes and cases. The objects are then decorated by the painters with scenes typically inspired by contemporary life in the USSR, but also by Russian history and folk traditions: landscapes; dancing girls; depictions from Russian tales such as Passynine's *Snow-white* or *The Little Red flower*; women in brightly coloured costumes; portraits of national heroes; copies of well known paintings; and of course the eternal *troikas* are to be found rendered in glowing colour.

To a large extent the revival of Russian papier-maché Easter eggs production today is due to the Sherimetev family. At the end of the eighteenth century this great landowning family possessed 100,000 'souls', as the expression ran. The Sherimetevs early adopted a liberal attitude towards their serfs and tried to install on their land an industry where these unfortunate 'souls' could work and earn some money. Count Sherimetev had himself married a serf, the actress Shemchugova, which perhaps explains his unusual magnanimity.

It was these land serfs who were the first to start the production of papier-maché boxes, thus creating a sort of cottage industry. This was to become the nucleus of the Vishniakov factory which was founded at the beginning of the nineteenth century. Success was slow at first, but the industry developed in parallel with the pan-Slavic movement and from then on its progress was rapid.

The Vishniakov factory seems to have produced Easter eggs in papier-maché from the very start, and in 1850 it was employing the services of eight craftsmen. By 1876, twenty painters and about 250 unskilled workers were busy in the factory. Round the 1880s, the inhabitants of a dozen or so villages on the outskirts of Moscow were engaged in the production of lacquer boxes and various Easter eggs, most of them destined for the Vishniakov factory. At about this time several other small factories started in Russia, but these all disappeared rapidly, except one, belonging to P. I. Korobov, who had started in Fedoskino in the last years of the eighteenth century with the help of German craftsmen from Brunswick in Germany.

At the beginning, the Korobov factory produced only cap vizors in varnished papier-maché for the military authorities. From vizors Korobov progressed to the production of snuff-boxes decorated with various Russian scenes. Then, around 1820, the factory came into the hands of Korobov's son-in-law, Peter Vassilievitch Lukutine, who immediately increased production, and always marked the objects with his own initials or with his name in Cyrillic lettering. From 1828, Lukutine obtained the right to mark his products with the two-headed eagle of the Romanovs, by kind permission of Tsar Nicolas I. The lids of the boxes of that era were often decorated with views of Moscow, but in 1843, under the influence of the emerging pan-Slavic movement, Lukutine, now helped by his son Alexander, began to decorate his papier-maché products with scenes and characters borrowed from Russian peasant life. The works of famous painters such as Jakowsky, Popov and Orlovsky were also reproduced at the Lukutine works.

It should be borne in mind, however, that only the lids were decorated, the boxes themselves being invariably in black lacquer. This was a deliberate decision intended to bring out the brilliant colours of the miniatures. Only occasionally were red, blue and white backgrounds used – although the Easter eggs often had red backgrounds. Towards the middle of the nineteenth century, Lukutine, followed incidentally by Vishniakov, produced two designs which became renowned, the *troika* and the tea drinkers' scene. These were reproduced thousands of times. Lukutine and Vishniakov also manufactured a very large number of papier-maché Easter eggs, sold on the home market cheaper than their porcelain equivalents, and more often than not decorated with biblical scenes, notably from the Passion of Christ.

Lukutine's great period of development was between 1840 and 1870, when the first effects of partial industrialisation were making themselves felt even in Russia. This change dealt a hard blow to traditional craftsmanship and marked the decline of the factory. The son, Alexander Petrovitch Lukutine, became director at the death of his father in 1867. He in turn was succeeded by his own son Nicolas, then director of the Philharmonic Society of Moscow and not much interested in the papier-maché work of his forebears. The Lukutine factory closed down in 1904. That was the end of a great era. Or nearly the end. For a few years later, in 1910, four craftsmen and six painters who used to work for Lukutine, founded an *artel* or cooperative society, the Fedoskino Centre, in order to restart the craft of lacquered papier-maché. Today, Fedoskino is a great centre for the production of lacquered papier-maché objects, but unfortunately Easter eggs have been left out of the production programme.

Apart from Palekh, Kholoui and Fedoskino, there are other centres in Russia which once made Easter eggs and where lacquered papier-maché is still produced, but information about them is very difficult to obtain. One centre at Mstera, near the town of Vladimir, was well known for its papier-maché Easter eggs at the end of the nineteenth century and at the beginning of the twentieth. Also celebrated was the craft centre of Gestovo, near Moscow, the origins of which go back to the first years of the nineteenth century.

Russian papier-maché eggs are very much sought after today, but they are difficult to find, as most of them, trinkets though they were, disappeared inside Russia. Vishniakov, Lukutine and the other manufacturers exported hardly any to the West. Indeed, their very rarity makes them the more desirable, especially since these souvenirs of Tsarist Russia are pieces of real craftsmanship.

Each egg took nearly four months to complete. Once the object was finished, the painter took over and began his work by drawing his design on paper. He then lifted the tracing on to the egg before starting the actual painting, the *roskrych*. The artist first applied blobs of paint on to the drawing, then proceeded to harmonise the colours. Then he reached the *plavi* (or glazing) stage as the old icon painters used to call it. The *plavi* was a liquid paint, heavily diluted with egg distemper. Once a harmonious colour combination had been found, the *propiss* was made, that is to say the contours of the drawing were traced using a deeper colour than the background, and a certain relief was given to the whole by the addition of light shadows. It still needed gilding.

Once the painter's work was finished, the egg was given back to the workshop for varnishing and polishing. The Lukutine eggs were generally covered with six or seven coats of varnish, which had to be rubbed down each time. Russian Easter eggs in lacquered papier-maché are always little masterpieces and should be treated as such. The only question is: 'Where are they to be found?'

A papier mâché Easter egg, composed of two sections, one half painted with St Nicholas, the reverse with the Resurrection, the interior with the mark of the Moscow Old Believers Community at the Cemetery of the Transfiguration, 4½in. (12cm.) long, late 19th century. *Courtesy: Sotheby's*

PORCELAIN EASTER EGGS
OF RUSSIA

Nobody will ever know for sure who was the first manufacturer to evolve the idea of producing porcelain Easter eggs. Some time in the second half of the eighteenth century, they began occasionally to appear, perhaps as the result of a worker's initiative. It is thought that porcelain egg production may have been started by the Russian Imperial factory in St Petersburg, which was opened on an experimental basis as early as 1744 under the reign of the Empress Elizabeth. But it was only under the reign of Catherine (1762–1796) that porcelain manufacture really got under way, thanks to the arrival in Russia of French, Austrian and German craftsmen who were specially recruited to teach their know-how to their Russian colleagues. This may explain why early Russian porcelain eggs are similar to the best Western production: in fact they do not seem Russian-inspired at all, for they bear a striking similarity to the wares produced in Meissen or Sèvres. It was only at the end of the century, after Georgi's book *Description of the races of the Russian empire* had been translated into Russian, that porcelain decoration began to adopt a definite Russian style, and St Petersburg started to produce the famous statuettes of Russian peasants, craftsmen, dancers and singers that are so keenly collected today.

The first Easter eggs, then, produced under Catherine II, were often embellished with floral designs and could almost as easily have been produced in Meissen or any other factory of Western Europe. But they did have something intrinsically Russian about them: they were each pierced through so that a ribbon could be attached to them. Most of them were the size of a hen or duck's egg, although some are near 20 cm in height. Such Easter eggs in porcelain were never produced outside their country of origin, except in the then Polish territories of Ukraine (now part of the USSR) and, as will later be explained, in Berlin.

Under Tsar Alexander 1 (1801–1825), the first all-Russian eggs appeared, decorated with scenes from the New Testament, scenes of the Passion of Christ, and figures of the saints of Holy Russia. All these were usually set against typical Russian landscapes with churches dominated by onion-shaped steeples. These designs tended to place the eggs in an older Russian tradition, quite different from the Russian empire style that was dominant at the time.

These eggs met with such success among the Russian people that other Russian manufacturers were soon following St Petersburg's lead. Among these successors was the Francis Gardner factory which lasted until 1891, when it was taken over by the Kutznetsov business empire. Founded at Verbilki, near Moscow, in 1756, the Gardner factory soon became the rival of the St Petersburg works. It was more commercially inclined, and produced vast quantities of Russian statuettes and groups. Modelled by local craftsmen, these pieces have original forms and typically bright Russian colouring. The Easter eggs produced by Gardner, however, like those of other Russian factories at the time, are not marked with the name of their place of origin: without the least shame, both St Petersburg and Gardner marked their wares instead with the cross-swords of Meissen, up to the first years of the nineteenth century. Around 1840 the Gardner factory started producing more vulgar wares and its years of greatness were over, although it went on making Easter eggs until the very end.

A large number of porcelain factories sprang forth in Russia in the early years of the nineteenth century, but Western historians have never given them the credit they deserve, due, no doubt, to the fact that Russian eggs rarely if ever reached Western markets. The sudden proliferation of manufacturers was due to an initiative taken by Tsar Nicolas I, who, starting in 1806, decided to impose a heavy tax on all imported porcelains. The same year, a German, Karl Milli, founded in Garhurovo, about fifty kilometres from the Gardner factory, what was to become the world-famous Popov works. Alexai Gavrilovitch Popov remained at the head of the firm until 1850 when it was taken over by his two children, Dimitri and Tatiana. The factory was sold in 1870 to a certain Zhukov, then to a German again, Rudolf Schroeder, who in turn sold it to a Russian named Kholatov. Its last owner, Fornichev, closed it finally in 1875.

Popov porcelain established its reputation in 1812, when it became immensely popular in Russia for its depiction of military battles, portraits of the heroes of the 1812 campaign against Napoleon's grand army, and peasant and village scenes.

The Popov statuettes are always very elegant, but it is difficult to identify any Easter eggs as Popov creations as, once more, the eggs are never marked. It might be guessed that eggs decorated with military scenes are of Popov origin, although this type of decoration was also used on eggs of Berlin manufacture. It would no doubt take an expert in militaria to distinguish between Russian and Prussian regalia and therefore, with confidence, render unto Caesar that which is Caesar's. In 1814, Prince Nikolai Brisovitch Youssoupoff founded his own factory in Archangelskoie, but it never reached a commercial level of production, remaining the whim of a rich aristocrat.

The works which was to become the most important porcelain production centre of all Russia, was founded in Novo-Kharitonovo in 1810, by a certain Kutznetsov for his two sons, Terentii and Anisim Kutznetsov. The expansion of the new concern was very rapid. One by one, with an astonishing sense of enterprise, the Kutznetsov family purchased other works until in 1889 they were able to form the M. S. Kutznetsov concern, responsible for two-thirds of the entire Russian porcelain production. In 1891, having bought up the Gardner factory, the Kutznetsov family were left in control of a vast business empire with production centres of porcelain located all over Russia. Most of these factories produced Easter eggs, but on a seasonal basis, and mainly during the second half of the nineteenth century.

Nikita Semonovitch Khrapunov founded his works in the village of Kuziaevo, near Moscow, as early as 1812. It expanded so rapidly that soon each of his sons Vlas, two Ivans, Abram, Gerasum and Osip could be placed in charge of his own works.

Another important firm was founded in 1820, in Volokitino, in the region of the Ukraine, by a certain Miklachevsky. He was a rich landowner who had discovered kaolin on his estate, and very cunningly concluded that by establishing a porcelain factory on his property he would be able to exploit not only the kaolin but also the cheap labour provided by his serfs. But Miklachevsky had to get

craftsmen from abroad to start production, including a man named Dart, a modeller from Sèvres, in France. The result was the production of obvious copies of Western European models. There are no reports of Easter eggs being manufactured here.

The Batenine factory in St Petersburg, founded around 1812, is known on the other hand to have made eggs. Serguei Batenine, a merchant, left the works to his son Filipp in 1829, who sold it three years later to one Kornilov. The Batenine creations are of the highest standard, always decorated with very bright colours and the pinky gilt which characterises Russian porcelain.

Between 1820 and 1830, the Safronoff works near Moscow begin to appear in the records. It produced not only first quality tableware, but a long series of typical Russian statuettes and some Easter eggs, all except the eggs marked with a peculiar letter 'C', which looks similar to the 'G' of Gardner.

Around 1830, two other manufacturing centres appeared near Moscow, that of Terekhoff and Kiselev and that of Kozloff, which produced mainly tableware, occasional statuettes and probably some Easter eggs.

In 1835, Mikhail Savinovitch Kornilov founded his first porcelain works in St Petersburg. Thanks to his success in attracting workers away from the Imperial factory and the Popov concern, his production was of the finest, right from the start, so much so that he won a medal at the 1839 Moscow Exhibition. The colours were rich and always heightened with gold, the motifs elegant. The success of Kornilov was such that he soon had to rent other factories to be able to keep up with the demand. From 1893 to 1917, when the factory closed down at the time of the revolution, the firm was known as 'Kornilov Brothers'. All the porcelain from the Kornilov factory is marked with the firm's name, in under-glaze red until 1861, when the serfs were liberated – which was a mortal blow to the porcelain industry – and afterwards in blue, also in under-glaze. Unfortunately during the last quarter of the nineteenth century the quality declined markedly and Kornilov ended up by producing cheap porcelain earmarked for the export market.

Between 1830 and 1840, there appeared yet another porcelain works in the village of Kuziaevo, near Moscow. It was founded by the brothers Ivan, Tikhon and Semen Novyi. Production at the

Kuziaevo works included conventional tableware, and other objects beautifully painted by local artists with flowers, views of Moscow, and portraits of Tsar Nicolas I and other celebrities.

A couple of years before the Novyi brothers arrived in the village, Peter Timofevitch Fomin had founded a small factory there, producing cheap porcelain intended for the poorer classes. Many other small firms, practically unknown today, existed solely to cater for the cheaper market, producing what the Russians call *traktir* (inn, or hotel) porcelain. Among these small factories, which are all thought to have put Easter eggs on the market, one finds A. T. Safronov, founded in 1830 in the village of Korotskaia and which lasted only about twenty years; Gouline, founded by Vassilii Gouline in the village of Friazevo, district of Bogorodsk, near Moscow; and Guzhev, another small firm in the village of Cherniatka, near Tver, which was sold to a certain S. I. Moslennikov in 1879. *Traktir* porcelain was also made by Sabanine, founded around 1850 in the village of Klimovka and kept in business until 1875; by the Barmin brothers, in Fryazino; by T. Gunther in Moscow, and by the firms of Mardacheff, Ovetchine, Moussoukov and Nassaonov. Those and some so far unrecorded porcelain manufactures produced millions of fairings, statuettes, groups and most likely Easter eggs, for the huge Russian market. Today those ephemeral Russian fairings are eagerly sought after by numerous collectors, because of their infinite charm, and their great originality.

The unstable state of Russian porcelain production was the key to the variation in quality of decoration one notices in the Easter eggs, some of which, painted by first-class artists, are almost perfect, while others show a certain amount of crudity in decorating technique. But it is difficult to remain unmoved at the sight of these eggs, both the good and the bad, for they all remind us of a near-forgotten era, of a Holy Russia of pealing church bells, of colourful feasts, of deep-voiced singers, the Russia of the Tsars, the Russia of the golden cupolas rising above the churches.

The liberation of the serfs, proclaimed in 1861, badly hit Russian industry, which had now to carry on without unpaid labour. Many companies were forced to close down. Yet it was after this, during the reign of Tsar Nicolas II, that some of the most beautiful Easter

eggs ever made were produced.

Russian eggs today are mostly to be found in museums, displayed in showcases where they can be admired for the originality of their decoration, for the message of faith they often convey, for the strength of the symbolism they represent, for a forgotten past they bring back. These faraway Russian artists decorated their porcelain eggs with an astonishing variety of images: with roses, petunias and pansies, with monuments from Moscow and St Petersburg, with country scenes, with biblical stories, with portraits of the saints, with floral wreaths in which they placed the monograms of the Tsar or the Tsarina, and the double-headed eagle of Russia. Some of them even carry geometrical designs and, occasionally, motifs inspired by the Art Nouveau movement.

Russian porcelain eggs, unfortunately, are extremely rare and much sought after. The painful result is that when they do appear on the market they fetch very high prices. Reproductions exist of course, for similar eggs have been made now and then for Russian exiles, mainly in the United States, but also in France and, if rumour is to be believed, even in England.

POLISH AND GERMAN EGGS IN THE RUSSIAN STYLE

~~~~~~

Many collectors imagine that all porcelain eggs that have been pierced in order to pass a ribbon through them, and are hand-decorated, are Russian. In fact, this is far from the truth, for both Poland and Germany once made very similar Easter eggs.

The Polish porcelain industry is indeed hardly known in the West. It is for instance seldom mentioned in the history books, that the Polish king, Stanislas Augustus, founded a porcelain company in Warsaw in 1774. This was the Belvedere factory, first placed under the management of a certain Schutter, who died in 1783. Another works founded by one Wolfe and also located in Warsaw, replaced the earlier firm and carried on the tradition of fine porcelainware laid down by Belvedere. These first Polish porcelain factories had an influence on the development of a third, in the district of Volhynie, a territory now integrated into the Russian Ukraine, but where, at the time, Polish culture predominated.

It was towards the end of the eighteenth century that Prince Gartorisky founded a factory on his estate at Koretz, in the district of Volhynie, at the head of which he placed a certain Mezer, a man of taste who had been previously connected with the Sèvres factory. In 1803, Merault, who also came from Sèvres, became administrator of the firm, when Mezer decided to set up on his own. The production of the two factories was sold in Poland and in the southern parts of Russia, which perhaps explains why they began to make Easter eggs in the Russian manner. The Koretz works marked all their articles with a stamp representing an eye in a triangle and sometimes with the name of the factory underneath. But the trade mark of the second firm at Baranovka, varied. Certain pieces carry the name of the village, others the name of Mezer and, very often, three stars. On top of this, when Baranovka assumed more importance in the porcelain industry, the Russian government granted it the privilege of marking

Porcelain marks on Easter eggs by Herend, Hungary and by Hammersley, Staffordshire

its products with the double-headed eagle of the Romanovs.

There were of course other factories at the time in Poland, but their products never equalled those from Koretz and Baranovka and, as far as is known, they never produced eggs, although this is not certain.

Baranovka produced an enormous quantity of porcelain Easter eggs during the nineteenth century, but mainly for export to the Russian market, which explains the regrettable absence of eggs from this factory in modern Polish museums. Polish porcelain eggs are in no way different from those produced by the numerous Russian factories and, as none of them are marked, it is very difficult to identify their place of origin unless there is a clue somewhere in the decoration, something particularly Polish, to identify a particular piece.

What complicates the situation for collectors even further is that there are also eggs that look remarkably similar to Polish and Russian ones that were produced neither in Poland nor in Russia, but in Germany. It was by a peculiar set of historical circumstances that such Easter eggs were produced by the Royal Berlin Porcelain Factory from about 1820 onwards. During the Napoleonic campaigns, the Tsar Alexander I and the King of Prussia, Frederick William III, became allies. The alliance was cemented when Frederick William's daughter, Princess Charlotte, married the Tsarevitch Nicolas in 1817, so that when he in turn became Tsar of all the Russias in 1825, as Nicolas I, his German wife became Empress Alexandra Feodorovna.

Berlin Easter egg.

Left: Very early Berlin porcelain Easter egg in the Russian manner, pierced to let a ribbon through, and decorated with views of Wartburg Castle. *Collection Gunter Rohloff, Berlin*

Right: Berlin porcelain Easter egg decorated with painted views of Berlin on a white background. The views are the Brandenburg Gate, the Museum built by K. F. Schinkel, in 1828, and the Long Bridge of Berlin. Circa 1830–1835. Height 6cm. *Collection Gunter Rohloff, Berlin*

The royal family of Prussia remained very close to their Russian relatives and, at the slightest opportunity, its members exchanged good wishes and presents. And the Empress Alexandra, although she lived in faraway St Petersburg, never ceased to remain attached to her native country. So the year following her marriage to the Tsarevitch Nicolas, she adopted a very old Russian custom then observed by the St Petersburg Court, and at Eastertide despatched Easter eggs to her father, the King of Prussia, and to her mother, Queen Louise.

Because of the unreliable state of the roads between Russia and Germany, and a practically non-existent postal service between the two countries, the Empress was deterred from sending natural dyed or even porcelain eggs, which would have reached Berlin in an extremely sorry state. So she contented herself with either wooden lacquered eggs or, more likely, lacquered papier-mâché eggs. What is particularly interesting is that her Easter eggs were decorated with views not of St Petersburg but of Berlin and Potsdam. It is possible that the lacquered papier-mâché egg held today in the 'Lacquer Museum' in Cologne is one of these. The egg is decorated in the form of two medallions with views of Babelsberg and of its castle. The village of Babelsberg is located near Potsdam, but the castle was built only in 1834, which means that if the egg was sent to the Berlin Court, it was not before that year. Prof Dr Erich Kollmann, who examined the egg and who is the author of the most definitive book on Berlin Porcelain, attributes to it a Russian origin. It might be remembered here that German craftsmen were engaged by the

Left: Berlin porcelain Easter egg decorated on one side with the scene of the crucifixion on a white background. The kneeling figures are those of the Virgin Mary and John the Evangelist. On the other side of the egg is depicted a golden chalice and the Host floating on a cloud. Both scenes are surrounded by a golden garland. Circa 1825–1835. Height 6cm. *Collection Gunter Rohloff, Berlin*

Right: Berlin porcelain egg decorated with leaves, flowers and golden tendrils. On one side a child sits upon a goat, playing a flute. On the reverse side is a scene of a swan flapping its wings. The two scenes are separated on each side by a flaming torch, and the extremities of the egg are decorated with leaves on a matt gold background. Circa 1825–1835. Height 6·5cm. *Collection Gunter Rohloff, Berlin*

Vishniakov firm, and that they may well have produced some eggs for their own families in Germany.

Whatever is the truth, the eggs sent to Berlin by Empress Alexandra seem to have created a strong impression at the Prussian court – so strong that the nearby Berlin Porcelain Factory, a state firm, began producing porcelain Easter eggs in the Russian style around 1820. Such Easter eggs, some of which could easily be mistaken for Russian ones, were made only in Berlin and nowhere else in Germany, no doubt because of the Prussian court's preference for Berlin. Meissen, far away in Saxony, the first and most important porcelain factory in Germany, did not produce a single egg.

Berlin eggs can often be distinguished from Russian ones by the

Left: Berlin porcelain scent bottle in the shape of an egg, decorated with the portrait of Frederic II in sepia Cameo. The medallion is surrounded by a border in gilt in slight relief, in Art Nouveau style. The porcelain stopper is in the form of a crown. Circa 1900. Height 7·5cm. *Courtesy Gunter Rohloff, Berlin*

Right: Berlin porcelain scent bottle in the shape of an egg decorated on a white background, with views of the Hohenzollern Castle at Hechigan. The border pattern is in Art Nouveau style, but the stopper is in brass. Circa 1900. Height 7·5cm. *Collection Gunter Rohloff, Berlin*

Berlin porcelain eggs from the first half of the 19th century, decorated with flowers on white background, heavily decorated with gold. *Courtesy: Staatliche Museen zu Berlin, DDR*

various types of decoration used. The majority of the Russian-style Berlin eggs measure two or three inches in height, and the scenes painted on them are often unmistakably German, leaving no doubt about their attribution. One finds German landscapes and German monuments, German castles and German military scenes – incongruous as these may seem on Easter eggs. But religious scenes, geometric designs and floral motifs make identification more difficult, so that they cannot always be told apart from their Russian models. Many Berlin eggs were decorated with handpainted roses, among other flowers. Most of the eggs have royal blue or light blue backgrounds, the scenes appearing in medallion form. They are generally enhanced with gilding of a slightly less pinkish shade than those from Russia.

Left: Easter eggs in Berlin porcelain with geometrical designs, heavily decorated with gold. Both are 4cm in height. First half of the 19th century. *Courtesy: Staatliche Museen zu Berlin, DDR*

Right: Berlin porcelain Easter eggs from the beginning of the 19th century, both 6cm in height, decorated with garlands of flowers in natural colours, the poles being decorated in gold. *Courtesy: Staatliche Museen zu Berlin, DDR*

Right: Two beautiful porcelain Easter eggs from the first half of the 19th century. The egg illustrated on the left side is decorated with a painting of the Madonna and child, thought to be a copy of an unknown Italian Renaissance painting. Height: 6cm. The other egg, 9·3cm in height, is decorated with a painting of an unidentified royal personage in prayer. *Courtesy: Staatliche Museen zu Berlin, DDR*

Left: Berlin porcelain Easter eggs, respectively 6·3cm and 6cm tall. *Courtesy: Staatliche Museen zu Berlin, DDR*

89

The great period of the Berlin eggs in the Russian style lasted a mere twenty years, from 1820 to 1840, the year in which Frederick William III died. But this fact should not deter collectors, for the production of these beautiful porcelain Easter eggs continued in Berlin until the outbreak of the First World War. Of course times had changed, the Empress Alexandra was only a memory and so were the Russian eggs. Berlin was making eggs of its own, which for once, fortunately, were marked. One example was a perfume bottle in the shape of an egg, the stopper forming a miniature imperial crown – though this was never a part of royal headwear in Germany. Others were *bonbonnières* which could be opened to reveal the inevitable chocolate drops. And eggs mounted on bronze to hide Easter presents, some of quite respectable dimensions, poured from the Berlin company benches. These were not of course for the sole benefit of the court, but for sale all over Germany. Following a trend which had developed in Europe when the egg began to lose its traditional power as a symbol, the Germans produced Easter eggs which could more accurately be called containers. Yet some of these Berlin eggs from the later period are of great beauty and would grace any collector's showcase.

Two Berlin porcelain Easter eggs decorated with antique figures. The egg on the left is 6·3cm in height, with the figure, painted on a white background, holding a branch of lily. The egg shown on the right hand side is only 5·5cm in height, light blue background. *Courtesy: Staatliche Museen zu Berlin, DDR*

Left: Russian porcelain egg decorated on both sides with birds in medallions surrounded by a floral garland. Second half of the 19th century. *Courtesy: Sotheby Parke Bernet & Co*

Right: Russian imperial presentation egg in porcelain, probably from the St Petersburg Imperial Factory as it bears the cypher of the Empress Alexandra Feodorovna. End of the 19th century. *Courtesy: Sotheby Parke Bernet & Co*

Centre: Typical Berlin porcelain egg dated 1830 decorated with a view of Weimar Castle. *Courtesy: Sotheby Parke Bernet & Co*

OTHER CERAMIC EASTER EGGS

~~~~~~

During the last quarter of the nineteenth century and at the beginning of the twentieth, small German concerns, mostly from the south of the country, started producing porcelain Easter eggs on an industrial basis, and exporting them in vast quantities to other countries. These were never a match for the artistic quality of the beautiful handpainted eggs of Berlin, since they were mostly transfer-decorated and their hard-paste was of a somewhat indifferent quality. They were also of course much cheaper than the Berlin eggs, and practically always moulded in two parts which fitted together to serve as a *bonbonnière*. They were sold in Germany and exported to confectioners all over Europe to be filled with sweets and chocolate drops and sold at Eastertide. Besides the two-piece *bonbonnière*, Germany produced standing eggs, de-capitated eggs with or without cover, and eggs mounted on cheap metal bases usually containing one or two small perfume bottles. The German factories also made millions of Easter 'fairings' of questionable quality, which seem later to have disappeared from the scene.

At the turn of the century, the firm of Carl Ens, in Volkstedt, was very active in this field, and many well moulded and decorated eggs were produced by its ovens. Around 1900, one of Ens' modellers, who probably knew more than the rest about the ancient meaning of Easter, had the fertile idea of producing pagan Easter eggs, from which all Christian association had been removed. Next to an upright egg painted with flowers, he placed a statuette of the Goddess of Spring and even went so far as to inscribe *Ostara* on the egg base, the ancient word from which derives the word Easter. It was the first time in modern history that the Easter egg had been deprived of its Christian or folkloric apparel.

The production of German Easter eggs has never really declined, for the demand has remained relatively buoyant, and even today firms such as the Rosenthal company in Bavaria are still going concerns. Another firm, Matthis and Ebel in Mabensdorf, founded in 1882, was responsible for the production of a considerable quantity of eggs. Several Bohemian porcelain firms also became involved in the movement from the end of the nineteenth century, and Czech museums will no doubt one day be sorry to have failed to secure a few of the best examples.

However, it was above all the porcelain manufacturers from the region of Limoges, in France, who inundated the market with Easter eggs, most of which cannot be attributed to a particular manufacturer as they are either unmarked or marked with a very simple 'Limoges, France' which gives a clue only to the place of origin. Limoges, from about 1875, produced eggs of practically every type,

Contemporary British Easter eggs in Coalport porcelain.

North of England earthenware egg; decorated on one side with under-glaze purple transfer of a dog and bushes, and over-glaze decoration of a flower in red, are painted in black. Probably made at Scott's Pottery, Southwick, Sunderland. *Permission of the Sunderland Museum*

some handpainted, some transfer-decorated with an unimaginable number of different scenes, many of them of definite eighteenth-century inspiration, even down to the everlasting *chinoiseries*. But Limoges also used the whole panoply of Easter lore for the decoration of its eggs: children, bunnies, church-bells, hares, chicks, and spring flowers. At present there are still two factories in Limoges producing eggs, many of which are put on the export market. One is the Manufacture Nouvelle de Porcelaine, a factory which has been in existence only for the past twenty years, and the other is the firm of Malbec.

Very indifferent porcelain eggs have been made in Belgium and in Holland, notably by the Gouda company. Hungary produced some interesting porcelain eggs, which are rarely seen outside the country: most of them, decorated occasionally with designs which recall the decoration of the dyed natural eggs, have come from the Herend company, which is located not far from Lake Balaton, a few miles from the town of Veszprem.

Eggs have also been made occasionally in earthenware, for instance in Belgium, Holland, Germany, and France. The Portuguese are responsible for many of these, which are always decorated with small flowers or in blue and white, the decoration being painted in rather faded tints, giving the eggs an ancient appearance.

Perhaps the nicest earthenware eggs a collector might hope to find, however, come from Britain. The production of these eggs, which have often nothing to do with Easter, was almost entirely confined to the far north of England. China eggs have traditionally been given there on various occasions, and it seems that miniature eggs containing 'frozen Charlottes' were given as presents to mothers of new born babies. In the north of England, beautifully decorated earthenware 'christening' eggs, hand painted or transfer decorated, were also offered to new born babies, with a pinch of salt and a piece of bread. These eggs were produced by local potteries. They were always painted with the baby's name and sometimes the date of his birth, as proved by the presence of such eggs in the Sunderland Museum and in some private collections.

The dates painted on the eggs indicate that the custom was more or less limited to the Victorian era. These eggs are always unmarked, with one single exception, that of those produced by William Walley, an obscure potter who ran a small firm in Shelton, Staffordshire. But other potters are known to have made eggs during the nineteenth century. Among them one finds Ball Brothers

White north of England earthenware egg, decorated with orange lustre and (in front) a purple over-glaze painted oval panel, with black border. 'John Hailes' is painted in black within. Ball Brothers pottery, circa 1860–1870. *Permission — Sunderland Museum*

One of a pair of north of England earthenware eggs, decorated with purple transfers of two young people skating. They are in East European costumes. One egg is marked 'John Clow' on the reverse side, the other 'Jane Clow'. Dawsons or Scotts, circa 1850. *Permission – Sunderland Museum*

of Deptford, and Scott Brothers, of Southwick, Sunderland. John Dawson, of the Lower Ford Pottery, in North Hylton, which closed down as early as 1864, also produced christening eggs, some in lustre ware, decorated sometimes with scenes having a definite East European flavour.

The answer to this mystery must lie somewhere inside the Dawson factory. How would the figures dressed in East European costumes on an egg now in the Sunderland Museum be explained? This egg is marked 'John Clow' and decorated in purple transfer with the figures of two young 'Russian' skaters. Dawson, incidentally, is also believed to have produced real earthenware Easter eggs.

Most of these north of England eggs are decorated with painted flowers, various scenic views, abstract patterns based on flowers and pine leaves, cupids in floral medallions, ships and even *chinoiseries*. The same potteries probably also produced those little eggs decorated with painted horses and foals which were sold as love tokens in the Victorian fairs of the north of England.

Ceramic eggs were hardly produced in Britain, as is proved by the total absence of eggs in the collections of the Stoke-on-Trent Museum, in the heart of the 'Potteries'. However, starting a few years ago and to meet an unexpected demand, such firms as Coalport, Wedgwood and the lesser known firm of Hammersley in Longton, Staffordshire, have been producing porcelain Easter eggs. These appear in the shape of *bonbonnières*, in two pieces, ready to

The 1977 Wedgwood Easter egg, in blue and white jasper, decorated with the dove of peace and a hand-applied garland of Easter lilies, and an embossed date motif. After twelve months, the original relief moulds will be destroyed. A new egg will be issued each year by Wedgwood. *Courtesy of Josiah Wedgwood and Sons Ltd*

A rather unusual Easter fairing, made in cream-ware and decorated with rare birds. Ducks are not very often associated with Easter.

be opened and filled with the sweets and chocolate drops, and practically always decorated with flowers. Wedgwood is issuing, from 1977, Easter eggs in jasperware. The subject chosen for the decoration of the first egg is the dove of peace, hand applied in low relief. Encircling the dove and the rim of the cover is a hand applied garland of Easter lilies, and there is also an embossed date motif. Each Wedgwood egg will be produced only for a period of twelve months. Then the relief moulds will be destroyed.

There is little doubt that contemporary collectors would above all prefer to seek the Russian and Berlin porcelain eggs, which unfortunately are now very rare. That preference is quite understandable and should be encouraged, as collections should be composed only of the best. This is rather easier to achieve for those who have the necessary financial means. But a collection of beautiful porcelain eggs produced in South Germany and in Limoges could be assembled at a reasonable price.

A final word of advice: collectors should know that a Parisian firm called Le Tallec has over the past few years produced exquisite hand-painted porcelain eggs, mounted on bronze and made after the eighteenth-century French style. Although these Easter eggs are obviously new, they have already become collector's items, all the more so because, unfortunately, it is likely that the Le Tallec firm, managed by a near-eighty-year-old gentleman, will soon be closed down.

THE RUSSIAN GOLDSMITHS' EASTER EGGS

The Easter festivities were always taken much more seriously in Russia than in the West. Easter arrives, in fact, at the summit of the orthodox year, and the event was of far more importance to old Russia than Christmas has ever been to the British. This example, of course, was set at the highest level, by the Imperial Court itself. The Russian Imperial family traditionally spent Eastertide in the Crimea, where the Imperial palace, doors wide open, became, for a day at least, a huge banqueting hall crowded with people. All the members of the imperial family, the courtiers, the servants and the members of the Imperial Guard were given Easter eggs by their Imperial Majesties. The eggs included humble *pissankis*, dyed and decorated natural eggs, handpainted wooden eggs, eggs in lacquered papier-maché, and porcelain eggs, sometimes carrying the monogram of the Tsar or of the Tsarina. Some were tiny eggs, smaller than a pigeon's, in wood, papier-maché or porcelain, which the Tsar gave to young girls and women to make into necklaces.

Starting in the second half of the nineteenth century, more costly eggs slowly made their appearance at Eastertide in court circles. Now eggs came encased in gold or silver. Silver gilt eggs containing painted icons were given, as well as eggs in precious metals covered with enamels in the old Russian style. Even the tiny necklace eggs were replaced by richer eggs in gold, in silver or in enamel. Of course, some beautiful eggs in precious metals, ornamented with precious stones, had already appeared during the eighteenth century, but these were rare, as is evidenced by the scarcity of such eggs in the museums of today. It was the Tsar himself, Alexander III, who really created a tradition whose extravagance would probably alone have justified the Russian revolution.

Around 1884, the Tsar Alexander III ordered an egg from Carl Fabergé, which he intended to give to the Tsarina Maria Feodorovna.

A famous 18th-century Easter egg belonging to the Danish royal family. According to a family tradition it was given by Duchess Charlotte of Orléans to Caroline, Queen of England, wife of George II. The ivory egg on the right hand side contains the small gold egg on the left, which in turn contains a hen in enamelled gold with brown spots, set with diamond eyes and a tiny crown set with forty diamonds and six pearls and a diamond ring. Although unmarked, this egg is French without any doubt. It is interesting to compare this egg with the first Fabergé Impérial egg of 1884, which consisted of an egg in gold enamelled white containing a yellow gold yolk, which in turn contains a tiny gold hen with two cabochon ruby eyes. The hen contained a tiny impérial crown, which in turn contained a ruby pendant. The two eggs, the 18th century one and the 19th century one, are very similar and one wonders if Fabergé did not get his inspiration in Denmark. *With the gracious permission of H.M. the King of Denmark*

This egg, the first to be produced by the great Fabergé, was not, as a matter of fact, as fabulous as those which were to follow year after year: externally it looked quite simple, in white enamel mounted on gold and about the size of a big hen's egg. However, the egg contained a gold yolk which could also be opened to reveal a miniature gold hen with two cabochon ruby eyes. And the hen in turn contained a miniature diamond replica of the imperial crown.

No one has ever been able to determine exactly how this particular artistic concept developed: more likely than not it was the Tsar's own idea. More certain is the fact that this very first imperial Easter egg, like all the others which were to follow, is not Russian looking at all. It is actually a pastiche of some of the eggs which had been produced in Paris and Augsburg during the preceding century and its style recalls the elegant forms of eighteenth-century France.

Many modern historians have reproached Fabergé for his imitations of eighteenth-century styles at a time when *fin de siècle* forms were dominating Western Europe, and in Russia on the other hand the goldsmiths were finding inspiration in the old Russian traditions. Yet Fabergé continued throughout his career to find his inspiration in the times of Louis XV and Louis XVI.

It has been suggested that his strange predilection for these early styles was due to his French descent, but this is very far fetched, as his ancestors had left France in 1685. Carl Fabergé himself was born 161 years later in St Petersburg. His father, Gustav Fabergé, had been at the time for four years the owner of a small goldsmith's workshop in the Bolshaya Morskaya. In 1860, Gustav left St Petersburg to settle in Dresden, Germany, leaving the workshop in the charge of his Finnish friend and partner, Peter Pendin. Young Carl, of course, visited his father and family in Dresden, stayed in Frankfurt and in England, passed through Switzerland and visited Paris, before going back to Russia, where he took over the family business in 1870.

From this point his story is one of extraordinary commercial success. He rapidly became the pre-eminent Russian goldsmith, appointed supplier to the Imperial Court in 1881. A year later his brother, Agathon, arrived from Dresden, joined him and probably influenced him more than is often thought. A goldsmith himself, Agathon had had more time than Carl to familiarise himself with the

A Carl Fabergé imperial Easter egg presented by the Empress Alexandra Feodorovna to her husband the Tsar Nicolas II, in 1913, on the occasion of the Romanov tercentenary. The egg opens to reveal a statue of Nicolas II on horseback. The top third of the egg is decorated with a latticed canopy encrusted with rose-diamonds, and rubies at each intersection. The push-button top is an emerald. One side of this egg, which is covered with pale green enamel on *guilloche* ground, is decorated with an applied diamond-studded double-headed eagle, with a fancy yellow circular cut diamond. The other side is decorated with a miniature portrait of the Tsarina flanked by the dates 1613–1913. *Courtesy of Christies, London*

Necklace of Russian Easter eggs, the four in the middle being by Carl Fabergé.
Courtesy: Sotheby Parke Bernet & Co

work – famous for its opulence and its meticulous detail – of the great German goldsmith, Dinglinger. Perhaps through Agathon, Fabergé acquired his own standards of technical perfection. In 1887, Fabergé opened a branch in Moscow, then others followed in Odessa, Kiev and, finally, London.

The revolution of 1917 marked the end of the Fabergé House, Carl himself managing to escape and take refuge in Switzerland where he died peacefully in 1920.

From 1884 onwards then, Fabergé made fabulous Easter eggs every year for the Tsar, one every year under the reign of Alexander III, then two under Nicolas II, for the last Tsar of all the Russias offered an egg not only to his wife, but also to his mother, the Dowager Empress. This sequence, over thirty years, was the most glittering series of decorated eggs ever conceived. The Resurrection egg, the Serpent Clock egg, the Danish Silver Jubilee egg, the Azova egg, the Caucasus egg, the Coronation egg, the Trans-Siberian egg, the Peter the Great egg, in all fifty-seven different Easter eggs, together make surely one of the most extraordinary collections of gifts ever created. These very special eggs are now scattered around the world, in museums as far apart as the Kremlin and the Virginia Museum of Fine Arts. Some are in the late Queen Mary's collection in Sandringham, others in various private collections in the United States and elsewhere. The last Fabergé egg of the imperial series to be sold in public auction, in the spring of 1977, reached the incredible price of 500,000 Swiss francs (about £125,000).

Apart from his imperial eggs, Fabergé also produced a series of eggs for less prestigious customers, such as Prince Felix Youssoupoff, Alexander Kelch and Doctor Emmanuel Nobel, founder of the Nobel prizes. In addition, Fabergé designed some cheaper eggs, to meet the

Right: This five-inch-high Coronation egg, by Fabergé, was presented to the Empress Alexandra Feodorovna by the czar Nicolas II of Russia. The red gold egg is enclosed by a green gold laurel leaf trellis, mounted at intersection with a yellow gold imperial eagle enamelled opaque black, and set with a rose diamond. Both ends of the egg are also set with diamonds. Inside this elaborate shell is concealed a replica of the imperial coach, used in 1896, at the coronation of Nicolas and Alexandra. The little coach is made of yellow gold and strawberry coloured enamel and surmounted by the imperial crown in rose diamonds and six double-headed eagles on the roof. The windows are engraved rock crystal, the tyres are platinum and the gold trellis is set with diamonds.

Two Fabergé imperial Easter eggs, belonging to H.M. Queen Elizabeth. On the left is the mosaic egg presented to the Empress Alexandra Feodorovna by Nicolas II, at Easter 1914. The skeleton consists of a system of gold belts to which is applied a platinum network set with diamonds and gems including sapphires, emeralds, topaz, quartz, rubies and demantoid garnets in flower patterns. The egg is divided into five oval panels by belts set with half pearls. Five brilliant diamonds are set at each intersection. The surprise inside the egg consists of a gold, pearl and translucent green

enamelled pedestal supporting an oval plaque, painted with the profiles of the five imperial children. On the right, an Easter egg by Fabergé, made for Barbara Kelch, in 1899. The Easter egg is enamelled in pale translucent pink and opaque white on a gold *guilloche* surface, with twelve reserve panels divided by broad bands of enamelled Indian roses and green enamelled leaves, set with rose diamonds. The surprise inside has been lost. *Reproduced by gracious permission of Her Majesty the Queen* demand that had arisen as the obsession with luxury eggs spread among the noble families of the empire. He made ovoid shaped *étuis* as well, and a large number of tiny 'necklace eggs', miniature eggs in precious or semi-precious stones mounted on gold, in enamel on *guilloche* ground, a technique very much in favour in the various Fabergé workshops.

Lately, the reputation of the Fabergé Easter eggs in the Western world has somewhat overshadowed the productions of other Russian goldsmiths, contemporaries of Fabergé. These artists, even though they produced less elaborate eggs than those of the master, at least have the merit of having turned out a sufficient quantity of eggs to attract a collector of more limited means.

Most of these lesser eggs were designed in accordance with the tendencies of the pan-Slavic movement, in the old Russian style, and are often adorned with *cloisonné* enamels on silver, silver gilt or gold backgrounds. These Easter eggs in precious metals emerged from the workshops of some of the most prestigious goldsmiths of the day, such as Ovtchinnikov, Ruckert, Sbinev and Kurliukev, who worked in St Petersburg, Moscow, Kostroma, Novgorod, Solvychegodsk and Rostov. Thousands of Easter eggs in silver and gold were also made by splendid craftsmen who worked in *artels*, or cooperative societies. They sold their finished articles to wholesalers such as Fabergé and Ovtchinnikov, who put them on the market. The names of these artists are unknown and will probably always remain so.

Besides Fabergé, the unchallenged master, it is the old Moscow goldsmith Paul Akimovitch Ovtchinnikov, active between 1851 and 1917 or thereabouts, who produced some of the finest Easter eggs. Ovtchinnikov was one of the leaders of the pan-Slavic movement in Russia, and his eggs were all in the old Russian style. He opened his first workshop in Moscow in 1851 and then a branch in St Petersburg in 1875. He was, above all, a master enameller, who found his inspiration in the works of his predecessors of the sixteenth and seventeenth centuries and in the old traditions of the Russian people. His work was intended solely for the Russian market, rather than for the international clientele Fabergé enjoyed. Ovtchinnikov never let himself be tempted by eighteenth-century sophistication. This attitude had its drawback: Westerners ignored him, for they did not appreciate the traditional Russian style with its

108

bright almost gaudy colours and its heavy appearance. Fortunately, Western connoisseurs have since had time to change their minds. Practically all the Easter eggs that came out of the Ovtchinnikov workshops are in enamelled silver, the enamels being applied by the *cloisonne* method. They are marked with the signature 'P. Ovtchinnikov' in Cyrillic lettering, and an imperial eagle.

Another contemporary of Fabergé, between 1890 and the revolution, was the talented enameller Feodor Ruckert, who worked exclusively in the old Russian style and is best known today for his production of tea caddies and Easter eggs. Feodor Ruckert was one of Fabergé's workmasters in St Petersburg, where he produced Easter eggs in silver gilt covered with *cloisonné* enamels painted with flowers and foliage. But his most famous eggs are in Chinese red enamels with Art Nouveau tree motifs. His eggs are marked with his initials in Cyrillic lettering.

A fourth silversmith well known for his eggs is Gregory Sbinev, who set up his own workshop in Moscow in 1893 and who worked only in Russian style. His ornate silver *kovschis* decorated with filigree enamels and cabochon precious stones are much sought after today. A collector of limited financial means can never hope to acquire a fabulous Russian egg by Fabergé or Ruckert, but he could well be in a position to obtain one of the thousands of silver Easter eggs made by other known and unknown Russian silversmiths, that

Russian silver Easter egg inscribed *'Kristos Voskresy'* (Christ is risen), made in Moscow at the end of the 19th century.

appear now and then in antique shops of the West. For it seems that most of the Russian silversmiths working at the end of the nineteenth century and the beginning of the twentieth at some time or other produced silver eggs. Probably, every silversmith who ever felt the influence of the pan-Slavic movement, such as Ivan Khlebnokol, who had a workshop in Moscow, or Orest Feodorovitch Kurliukev, was guilty of producing eggs! One such specialist in enamel work was Jacob Feodorovitch Mishukev, also of Moscow, whose creations remain accessible to collectors. With luck, too, it may be possible to discover eggs from firms such as Sazykov, founded in Moscow in 1793, or Maria Semenova, of Moscow, who worked in the old Russian style and employed up to 100 craftsmen in her workshop between 1890 and 1910.

Several unknown Russian silversmiths whose marks are not recorded anywhere, even in Russia, have produced what might be called silver *pissankis*, humble Easter eggs made of silver, which could be unscrewed. They were engraved with floral or geometric motifs and the words *Kristos Voskresy*, in Cyrillic lettering – the words that the old Russians said to one another when they met on Easter Sunday. Some of the Russian eggs, standing on a pedestal, could be unscrewed to form two useful egg-cups. Some other, rarer eggs can be opened by two little doors on one side of the shell to reveal a beautifully painted icon. Then, too, thousands of 'necklace eggs', always unmarked, were produced by Russian craftsmen in gold, silver, silver gilt and in enamel, in precious and semi-precious stones. These tiny eggs are so small that they may well be overlooked at an auction.

Collectors should know that most of the Easter eggs they are likely to come across will be hallmarked. Russian gold is marked with the assay mark *56*, while silver is usually marked *84*, sometimes *88*, for the ancient measure in use in Russia until 1925 was the *solothnik*, worth $\frac{1}{96}$th of the Russian pound of 409,5174 grammes, pure silver containing therefore 96 *solothniks*. Most of the hallmarks on Russian Easter eggs are covered by the *ukase* dated 9 February 1882, which stipulated that all silver articles had to be marked, except those of a weight inferior to half a *solothnik*. The usual standard met is *84*, the minimum allowed.

On small silver articles of Russian origin one usually also finds the maker's initials and the town mark, alongside the assay mark. The law required that silver articles be stamped with the assay mark, the maker's initials, the mark of origin or town mark and the date mark, plus the first letter of the Russian word for silver. But Russian made Easter eggs have also often been found stamped with added Polish hallmarks. The articles made by the *artels*, cooperatives created before the revolution to compete with the mass production of big firms, are usually stamped with the mark or the number of the *artel* itself. One often finds Easter eggs stamped for instance *A 11*, which means that they were made by *artel* No 11, in Moscow.

Russian Easter eggs in gold, silver and enamel, like practically all the objects made in Tsarist Russia, seem to have an irresistible appeal. They are very much sought after, as they are souvenirs of a Holy Russia which no longer exists, of a period which glitters mysteriously in the minds of many people, whose romanticism no doubt enables them to forget the hardships of the common people of the vast Tsarist empire.

NOVELTY EASTER EGGS

〜〜〜〜〜〜〜〜〜〜〜〜〜〜〜〜〜〜〜〜〜〜〜〜〜〜〜〜〜〜〜〜〜〜〜〜〜〜

Very few people indeed can hope to assemble a prestigious collection consisting only of Russian and German porcelain eggs, or of eggs made by the great silversmiths of Tsarist Russia and by their predecessors, the Augsburg goldsmiths. But most people, even of limited financial means, can afford the novelty eggs, unpretentious but always pretty, which have been made on an industrial scale in various countries, mainly France and Germany, from the middle of the nineteenth century onwards. For the commercialisation of Easter really started around 1850, when the confectioners realised the possibilities of the pagano-Christian feast. They began to produce eggs of all shapes and sizes, some reaching enormous proportions, made of sugar and marzipan, and filled with sweets. Chocolate was to come later. Other manufacturers, sensing that the fashion was catching on, started making container-eggs in every kind of imaginable material, such as wood, cardboard, glass and porcelain, each of which could be opened to reveal little presents, from cheap toys to expensive jewels.

In villages all over the continent, including Victorian England, of course, people continued to dye and to decorate natural eggs as they had done for centuries. But the townsfolk, in their urban hurry, were tempted by the beautiful novelty eggs displayed in the shop windows at Easter. The French writer Eugène Cortet could write the following in his book *Essai sur les fêtes religieuses*, published in Paris 1867:

'. . . but in the towns, luxury has put its stamp on the old custom and now, instead of offering the primitive egg, I mean the hen's egg, which is found nowadays only in the vulgar shop of the wine merchant, one offers eggs made in plaster, in sugar or any other substance. In those eggs which open, and the prices of which vary enormously, one finds tiny porcelain or tin miniatures, tiny pieces of furniture in pine or rose-wood, pink dolls, white Jesuses, masterpieces of patience coming from Germany. Sometimes it's a complete house or a bride's trousseau with wedding presents, diamonds and cashmere. In a confectioner's shop window, we have noticed the presence of a pretty toy which recalls the childish legend of the church bells during Holy Week. There are little belfries in bronzed cardboard, tied with ribbons, on which one can read: ''Easter, return from Rome''.'

There was no question about it, the merchants were already well established in the Temple. And the idea of the egg as a symbol, pagan or Christian, had been discarded, at least in urban districts. Easter had already become little more than a question of selling and advertising. In Britain the commercialisation of Easter was no less than on the Continent. Henry Cremer, toy seller of Regent Street, London, could advertise in 1874 that he sold Easter eggs containing minute glasses or tea-sets and even one containing 'a dolly and a dolly's trousseau'.

A well known wooden egg of the period contained a tiny jointed

Easter postcard 1911.

Easter postcard from about 1910, showing cardboard Easter eggs covered with silk printed floral motifs.

wooden doll about one inch high, advertised as the 'smallest doll in the world'. At the same time, a small china egg containing a little china 'frozen Charlotte' was on sale in Continental shops: it is possible that this type of egg was given not at Easter, but as a present to new-born babies.

All those toys – for after all they were nothing else but toys – were probably the same type as those that Eugène Cortet had reported in Paris ten years earlier. The toy egg was a German invention developed around the middle of the nineteenth century and exported to all European countries, together with the other famous German toys from Bavaria, Saxony, the south Tyrol and, of course, Nuremberg. The confectionery egg, which became fashionable on the Continent a few years before the start of the Franco-German war of 1870, reached Britain some years later, introduced from France and Holland. Of course, these masterpieces of confectionery, made of sugar, chocolate, marshmallow or marzipan are, naturally, beyond

114

Early 20th-century Easter card, showing decorated cardboard eggs.

French Easter card, 1913.

Kellemes húsvéti ünnepeket

Modern   Hungarian
Easter card.

Right: Two Belgian glass eggs from the end of the 19th century, painted with the names of the bride and the bridegroom. More than Easter eggs they were love tokens which couples used to exchange. *Collection Wery, Liège*

the reach of collectors. All of them were duly eaten. Only the container, if there was one, was left to survive, and that not usually for long.

Eggs were made in transfer-decorated tinware, wood, porcelain, earthenware, glass and in wicker-work. The porcelain egg became a fairing, usually of cheap quality, overburdened with hares, bunnies, chickens, cupids, little girls and little boys. These soon composed the Easter panoply, taken up at the end of the century by the picture postcard manufacturers (another German idea). But this naive little world of the fairing does remain a realm where collectors of Easter eggs can still search for and sometimes find unusual pieces for the price of a few pounds. They look lovely when they are displayed carefully in showcases.

Glass Easter eggs have a special appeal for two main reasons; they are much rarer than the porcelain ones, and most of them are of good quality. They were manufactured mainly in Germany, France and Bohemia, but also in Russia. Czechoslovakia has produced some beautiful glass eggs of the 'Mary Gregory' type, most often in ruby or cranberry glass, but also in rose, blue, turquoise green and amber glass, always decorated in white enamel with figures of children. The name 'Mary Gregory' was given to this type of cheap glass, because a certain painter on glass of that name was employed by the Boston and Sandwich glassworks, around the middle of the nineteenth century. But 'Mary Gregory' glass had been made before that time in Czechoslovakia, mainly by the Hahn Glassworks in Jablonec, the centre of production of glass jewellery.

The Czechs did not manufacture only Easter eggs in that style, but also drinking glasses, vases and jugs. These were always decorated with scenes in white enamel of children at play, and well-behaved young girls or little boys chasing butterflies. Czechoslovakia never stopped producing glass eggs, and even today one can find Czech eggs in solid iridescent glass. Italian ones, made in Venice, are also worth collecting. The nicest of these are of the paperweight type.

The Russians also produced Easter eggs in glass at the end of the nineteenth century and the beginning of the twentieth, the production having stopped abruptly at the time of the revolution. These eggs, which look almost exactly like their porcelain models,

Left: A few items of the Polish Easter panoply: painted eggs, Easter postcards decorated with decoupages and sticks made out of dried flowers from the region of Lowicz. *Polish Interpress Agency*

Four different Easter fairings.

Right: Modern Italian paperweight-type Easter egg in glass.

were in fact a cheaper substitute and were sold at Eastertide in fairs and village shops.

Russian glass eggs, which would be a delightful addition to any collection, have retained their symbolic meaning, which the Western fairings have long lost. They are not mounted, but are usually equipped with a thin suspension chain at one end and a tiny cross attached to a smaller chain at the other. Most of them are decorated with the initials '*KB*' (Christ is Risen), hand-painted in gold.

French has produced some beautiful opaline eggs of various pastel shades, sometimes decorated with painted flowers. Many are mounted on bronze nests or installed in tiny brass carts. But it is practically impossible to locate all the glass manufacturers who produced eggs during the second half of the nineteenth century, as production of this type of article was limited each year to a very short period, and often followed the craftsman's individual fancy.

Although the crystal-makers of Val Saint Lambert in Belgium are not particularly well known for their production of eggs, one can now and then find beautiful examples of Easter eggs in solid cut crystal of various colours made at the factory near Liège. To leave no doubt as to their purpose, these eggs are decorated with a hand-painted '*Joyeuses Pâques*' (Happy Easter).

Cardboard eggs, in two pieces, appeared at the very end of the nineteenth century, first in Germany and everywhere else immediately after. These eggs were to replace the more expensive types, such as those made in wood or tinware. The pioneers of the cardboard Easter eggs were however confronted with a difficulty when they got to the decorating stage: the decorative paper used to cover the mould, printed flat, would not fit the convex structure of the egg. This problem was overcome by cutting the paper in strips about an inch wide, then glueing them one by one on the egg, the decorative motifs being reconstructed as well as possible. These ordinary cardboard eggs, covered with bright printed paper, are still being manufactured in Germany. They can be found with all types of motifs, the most sought-after being those decorated with Art Nouveau or Art Deco figures. These were a refreshing change from the interminable and unimaginative hens, hares, bunnies and little boys and girls. Between the two world wars, some eggs were even decorated with Walt Disney characters. But the most difficult to find

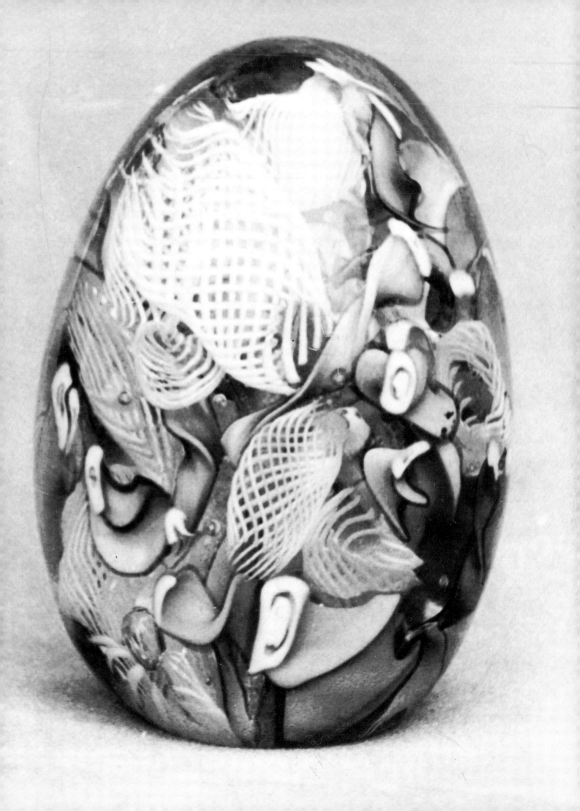

today are those cardboard eggs which were covered with various types of fabric, most usually silk, which were then either hand-painted and signed by the artist or more simply transfer decorated. Some of these eggs were also decorated with *découpages*. Some very rare French eggs were made of cardboard covered with kid, on which artists painted eighteenth-century-type scenes.

It should be noted, however, that old cardboard eggs are not as easy to find as one might imagine, for most of them have suffered over the years the fate of all trinkets of little value.

Apart from cardboard eggs, one might hope to find tiny wooden eggs containing minute rosaries, which were offered to little girls at Easter in most of the Catholic countries. Other eggs made of turned wood with hollow interiors, whose two halves could be unscrewed, reveal a compartment containing needles, thimbles and thread. These are not strictly Easter eggs, although they started out this way around 1870.

Rare glass Easter egg of the Mary Gregory type, decorated in white enamel on pink glass with a scene of a young boy chasing butterflies. Probably Czech, from the end of the 19th century.

Little dolls carrying Easter eggs on their backs, from Czechoslovakia.

Despite the fact that natural eggs dyed or decorated were so little regarded in the Western world, and preference was shown very early for artificial container-eggs, people in the villages, not only in Eastern countries but also in the West, continued serenely to dye their eggs at Easter. Only in a few places did the skill develop into an art: in most places it remains only part of a dying folklore.

Today the custom of giving eggs at Easter is still being practised, though its ancient meaning is almost completely forgotten. Eggs are given to children instead of toys or sweets, but they have rarely the magic that once attached to them. We have all lost that magic, if we live in the overcrowded conditions of towns and cities today. We have all lost a certain kind of community, and we are no longer in touch with mother Nature.

Polish painted Easter eggs. *Polish Interpress Agency*

But for this very reason, it would seem not a bad idea to save for the contemporary world some Easter eggs of long ago, even if they belong only to the time when our own mothers were teenagers.

This lady is one of the best known Hungarian decorators of Easter eggs and she has shown her skill in many Hungarian exhibitions organised abroad.

Two peasant girls from the region of Lowicz, in Poland, are busy decorating natural eggs. On the table, a tree made of paper, is a reminder of the awakening of nature. *Polish Interpress Agency*